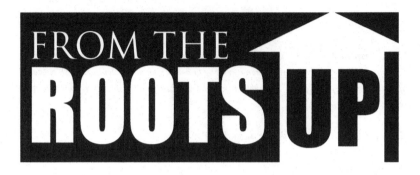

FROM THE ROOTS UP

A Collection of Thoughts on Life, Faith, and Politics

Randy Camacho

iUniverse, Inc.
Bloomington

From the Roots Up
A Collection of Thoughts on Life, Faith, and Politics

iUniverse books may be ordered through booksellers or by contacting:

iUniverse
1663 Liberty Drive
Bloomington, IN 47403
www.iuniverse.com
1-800-Authors (1-800-288-4677)

ISBN: 978-1-4759-6364-9 (sc)
ISBN: 978-1-4759-6366-3 (hc)
ISBN: 978-1-4759-6365-6 (ebk)

Printed in the United States of America

iUniverse rev. date: 01/03/2013

To Mom, Dad, and my sister Diane

CONTENTS

Introduction .... *xix*

CHAPTER 1—Family and Community 1

Freedom's promise shines in many ways 1
A tale of three brothers 2
The courage of compromise 7
Patriotism trumps dogma 9
Death came like a dove—gently and peacefully *11*
A nation of profilers 12
Miracle Diane 15

CHAPTER 2—Treasured Memories 20

Canals evoke memories of a simpler time 20
Family memories released in aroma of soup 21

CHAPTER 3—A Different Set of Lenses 24

Cope by putting life events in perspective 24
Stop and gain perspective 26

CHAPTER 4—The Wonder of Faith 30

Despite tragedy, faith guides retiring deacon.................. 30
Wrestler's faith prepares coach for end......................... 31

CHAPTER 5—Learning Moments..........34

History lesson invokes uneasy feelings in class Part I.... 34
Let moral compass not others guide your principles
    Part II..................36
One person's generosity makes another ponder
    right reaction....................37
Life's learning moments precious, must be seized......... 39

CHAPTER 6—Inspirational Stories 41

Old wrestler revives dream of competing.................... 41
Here's to celebrating non-traditional views 43
Tolleson's new vice mayor lives life by the moment....... 44
From a funeral-home manager: Life is precious............. 46

CHAPTER 7—The Faces of Immigration 48

A death in a family, a change in perspective................... 48
Happy Samuel's final word of the day: Adios!................ 49
Couple caught in the immigration maze....................... 51

CHAPTER 8—Political Philosophy/Strategy 53

We have plenty in common, so let's talk 53
Getting past gatekeepers isn't easy............................. 54
Civil disobedience is a peaceful way to fight injustice.... 56
Dems need to shift strategy 58
'None of the above' should be an option on ballot....... 59
Next U.S. senator needs passion, positive outlook......... 61
'The Process' can be deadly 63

CHAPTER 9—Politics in Arizona 65

It shouldn't be a crime to be a Good Samaritan............. 65
Feel-good legislation doesn't help—it hurts................... 66

Mixed messages a smoke screen for hypocrisy 69
Immigration reform: Arizona can lead the way 70
A peaceful backlash against hate 72
Franks isn't doing his job 74
A magical vision solves our transit problem 75

CHAPTER 10—Arizona's Education Conflict **77**

Schools are on right path 77
It's war: Education in Arizona under attack 78
We must fight Legislature's assault on teachers 80
Sober reality faces public education if tax fails 82
Overrides needed to help keep schools afloat 83

CHAPTER 11—Informational Columns **85**

Annoyed by military recruiters? Teachers' tour
   of Navy bases offers lesson 85
New Life helps abused end cycle 86
Blog keeping readers up to date on politicians 88
Several tips can help ward off dog attacks 89

CHAPTER 12—Sports **92**

Glendale council has earned right
   to Super Bowl freebies 92
Let's hope W. Valley, Cards don't rest on laurels 93

CHAPTER 13—Teen Challenges **96**

Teens engaged in 'sexting' could find
   futures derailed 96
Cell phone text messaging: Latest classroom
   disruption 98
As gang activity rises . . . rise again to snuff it 99

CHAPTER 14—The Slippery Slope 101

It's time to get angry about photo-radar abuse 101
More to red-light cameras than proponents reveal 102
Better engineering, fewer red-light woes 104
Will pensions come crashing down? 105
Medical marijuana initiative may open
   Pandora's box 106

CHAPTER 15—Offbeat Stories 109

Lent perfect time to try Tolleson fish restaurant 109
Monument atop hill reminds that past
   shapes us today 110
Jolly Old Elf Drove a Cop Car 112

CHAPTER 16—What's Race Got to Do With It? 114

Little Johnny at the Principal's Office 114
Do you ever feel sorry for White people? 116

PUBLISHED COLUMNS DATE LIST

Will pensions come crashing down?	(July 8, 2005)
Girl's death may shake views on immigration	(July 27, 2005)
Cell phone text messaging: Latest classroom disruption	(August 14, 2005)
Couple caught in the immigration maze	(September 14, 2005)
The Process' can be deadly	(October 8, 2005)
Jolly old elf drove a cop car	(December 21, 2005)
Franks isn't doing his job	(January 25, 2006)
Lent perfect time to try Tolleson fish restaurant	(March 1, 2006)
Death came like a dove—gently and peacefully	(March 29, 2006)
A peaceful backlash against hate	(April 15, 2006)
More to red-light cameras than proponents reveal	(May 6, 2006)
Despite tragedy, deacon has found his way with faith that doesn't waiver	(May 31, 2006)
New Life helps abused end cycle	(July 26, 2006)
Blog keeping readers up to date on politicians	(September 15, 2006)
Here's to celebrating non-traditional views	(February 9, 2007)
A magical vision solves our transit problem	(March 9, 2007)
Wrestler's faith prepares coach for end	(April 4, 2007)
Better engineering, fewer red-light woes	(May 11, 2007)
'Cashing in' is not very easy and change is forthcoming	(June 9, 2007)
Annoyed by military recruiters? Teachers' tour of Navy—bases offers lesson	(July 18, 2007)
One person's generosity makes another ponder right reaction	(August 4, 2007)
Tolleson's new vice-mayor lives life by the moment	(December 5, 2007)
Happy Samuel's final word of the day: Adios!	(January 12, 2008)

Glendale council has earned right to Super Bowl freebies (January 26, 2008)

Canals evoke memories of a simpler time (February 16, 2008)

History lesson invokes uneasy feelings in class (part 1) (March 22, 2008)

Let moral compass not others guide your principles (part 2) (March 26, 2008)

Several tips can help ward off dog attacks (May 24, 2008)

Getting past gatekeepers isn't easy (June 7, 2008)

Cope by putting life events in perspective (August 6, 2008)

It's time to get angry about photo-radar abuse (October 4, 2008)

Family memories released in aroma of soup (November 28, 2008)

As gang activity rises . . . . rise again to snuff it (December 31, 2008)

Let's hope W. Valley, Cards don't rest on laurels ((February 4, 2009)

From a funeral-home manager: Life is precious (March 14, 2009)

Teens engaged in 'sexting' could find futures derailed (April 10, 2009)

Old wrestler revives dream of competing (June 3, 2009)

Monument atop hill reminds that past shapes us today (July 4, 2009)

Feel-good legislation doesn't help—it hurts (August 24, 2009)

Mixed messages a smokescreen for hypocrisy (December 18, 2009)

We must fight legislature's assault on teachers (January 27, 2010)

Overrides needed to help keep schools afloat (February 23, 2010)

It's war: Education in Arizona under attack (April 9, 2010)

Sober reality faces public education if tax fails (May 12, 2010)

We have plenty in common, so let's talk (June 4, 2010)

Immigration reform: Arizona can lead the way (June 19, 2010)

Medical marijuana initiative may open Pandora's Box (July 23, 2010)

Civil disobedience is a peaceful way to fight injustice (September 15, 2010)

Dems need to shift strategy (November 27, 2010)

Next U.S. Senator needs passion, positive outlook (March 26, 2011)

Freedom's promise shines in many ways (July 2, 2011)

Life's learning moments precious, must be seized (March 30, 2012)

'None of the above' should be an option on ballot (July 29, 2012)

PREFACE

When the spirit moved me to write this book, I felt somewhat embarrassed. I deliberately added to that side of self-consciousness by naming the file holding the words to this book as *Memoirs*. Now, the word memoir seems reserved for famous people or those of extreme influence. So why would a common everyday person such as me write a memoir? It's simple, because it's uncomfortable. And being in a state of 'uncomfortable' in mind and spirit is a great motivator. It forces you to take on your insecurities or be defeated by them.

This state of uncomfortable compels you to tap into the senses that lay dormant even numb from the everyday grind of menial tasks. When I'm uncomfortable, I feel alive, truly alive.

It's important to understand that a memoir is simply an account of one's personal life and experiences. Sometimes the experiences are unpleasant, but as author C.S. Lewis pointed out, all that occurs in our life, both good and bad, shape who we are. Fate is like a sculptor. It carves out character one fine line at a time.

My life has been a series of hopes, trials, victories, and defeats. I wouldn't want it any other way. I'm not sure what lies around the bend, but I do know that since childhood, I've been fascinated by the world around me. And I'm just as captivated today as I was growing up when Dad allowed me to speak my mind about various topics as we drove to and from church. He would listen intently then correct me if I was wrong. Like the time shortly after the 1972 presidential election when Republican Richard

Nixon trounced the Democratic candidate, George McGovern. Assuming the Republican Party was the party of the rich, I said, "Well now we know there are more rich people than poor." Dad shook his head incessantly. "Oh No!" he stated emphatically. "There are many more poor people than there are rich!" Confused, I asked, "Then how is it that Nixon won?" Dad looked away and thought for a moment, then looking straight ahead at the empty road, he said, "Because many poor people don't vote!" That was a difficult notion for a child like me to understand. Wouldn't poor people have more reason to vote than the rich? I wondered.

Shortly after my congressional run in 2004, I received a call from Joel Nilsson, an opinion writer for the *Arizona Republic*. I had gotten to know Joel while he was a member of the newspaper's editorial board, the group that, in part, endorses political candidates running for office. In both my 2002 and 2004 campaigns, I was fortunate to receive its endorsement for the primary and general elections.

I was pleasantly surprised when I received Joel's phone call. He asked, "Hey Randy, our paper is looking to introduce a community paper that will go along with the regular paper. We want to offer what many community papers are offering across the state, a personal touch. Would you be interested in becoming a community columnist to offer your thoughts on the issues of the day?" Excited, I agreed. He promised a stipend for each column, but I never requested compensation. The way I saw it, I thought the *Arizona Republic* was doing me a favor by giving me a platform to express my thoughts. Since 2005, I've written columns on various topics, ranging from the political to touching stories of everyday life; each has inspired me to share them with you.

This book is a collection of vignettes of the diverse stories and thoughts I have written over the years. The columns are presented as they appeared in the *Arizona Republic* with the exception of a few edits that were necessary to maintain their spirit.

I chose these particular columns because they rendered the most response from the public and because, I believe, they provide the best insight of how I view life, politics and the world around us. There is also a compilation of thoughts and personal stories published only in this book.

I invite you to visit www.randycamacho.com for further information. Thank you and enjoy!

Best,
Randy

ACKNOWLEDGMENTS

Robin Everding Brown (Finance Director during my congressional run): Thanks for your loyalty and for fighting the fight. You made call time (fundraising) a fun experience.

Lynn Caddell (Long-time friend): I'm blessed to have you as a friend. Thanks for the great times, especially our weekly dinners on Thursday nights. I hope one day you decide to move back to the desert. I miss your wit and wisdom.

Jeff Eccles: You are the most ethical person I've ever known. Thanks for the practical jokes and for being my colleague all these years.

Mr. Finch (High School English Teacher): It's because of you that I have a love for writing. Thank you for not judging me and for giving me the opportunity to express myself unconditionally.

Adolfo Gamez: Thanks for your unwavering support. I know I can always count on you.

Father Joe Hennessy—Your devotion to the youth in our community during my teen-aged years was unparalleled. I will always appreciate how you made Bible study interesting and thought-provoking. Thanks for being a friend I could talk to.

Bob Hensler (Long-time friend): Much of what I've learned in life, I learned from you. Your faith inspires me.

Steve Knight (Former high school principal)—It was a privilege working with you. You taught me the true art of leadership.

Richard Krepel (High School Basketball Coach): You promised me my freshman year that I'd have a jump shot by my sophomore year. You worked diligently with me over the summer in our hot gym. You kept your promise.

Dr. Charles A. Landis: I realize I caused you much aggravation that it took me so long to earn my college degree. Your thoughtfulness and constant support will forever be etched in my soul.

Sean Laux (Friend/advisor): Your wisdom is beyond this world. Thanks for your advice and forward-thinking prowess.

Armando Macias (Long-time friend and campaign manager during my congressional run): You and I have journeyed together on the political road. I could not have travelled as far without you.

Reyes Medrano: Thanks for being a great mentor and Little League coach.

Maria Salas (High School Guidance Counselor): I never properly thanked you for your support as my guidance counselor. Thank you for your positive outlook and belief in me.

Jan Stone (College Advisor): Thanks for not letting me off the hook and for convincing me to register for college before I stepped out of your office.

A special thanks to Duke Photography
www.dukephotos.com

The Young Man that Could

In the spring of 1974, my eighth-grade baseball team at Tolleson Elementary, prepared to play our rival—Underdown Junior High. That team was loaded with talent, and undefeated to boot. Their uniforms were new and nicely pressed. Ours, on the other hand, were torn and tattered. Our baseball team doubled as a slow-pitch softball team, which many experts will tell you are a bad combination. The habits one picks up in softball—like dropping your elbow before swinging your bat—haunt you in baseball where the pitch comes at you much faster and at a different angle. Our team was a work in progress. We were excited, though, that the game would take place on our home field.

The day prior to the game, we wrapped up practice and huddled around our coach, Gary Mendenhall. Someone asked Coach Mendenhall if anyone had ever hit a homerun at Unit One, the park where we played our games. Kicking the tip of his bat with his right toe, as he often did, our coach said, "In my many years of coaching, I've seen some of the best players that I think I'll ever see and if none of them could hit the ball out of the park, no one will!" It was hard to disagree with Coach Mendenhall, especially since there was a 30-foot net towering above the original fence.

At that moment, however, my mind instantly travelled to the land of possibility. I imagined a homerun ball catapulting out of the ball park then bouncing on the street passed the fence. It then propelled upward onto the rooftop of a brick house across the street eventually settling on the lawn. Deep in my soul, I felt a homerun was possible but I was not about to openly disagree with my coach.

Game Day quickly arrived. Fans squeezed together in the small stands while others watched from their cars. My turn to bat came in the second inning. The pitcher had a tremendous curve ball; I fell victim to it for a strikeout. The more I thought of my striking out, the harder I pounded in my glove. I was anxious for my next shot at the pitcher. That would come a few innings later.

Once again, the curve ball was getting the better of me. Down two strikes, I gambled that the next pitch was going to be a fastball. Instinctively, I made myself believe that. Every fabric of my being prepared for a fast ball; I risked looking a fool if it wasn't. Guessing correctly, the fastball came down the pike straight and hard. I swung with great conviction. I didn't feel a thing when my bat made contact with the ball. I saw it shoot straight into the sky, like a firework. In my mind, a fly ball to be caught in the outfield. Still, I ran hard and just as I rounded first base, I looked toward left field only to see the outfielder removing his cap as if saluting the ball he was helpless to catch. Everyone felt the historic moment as the ball sailed over the fence and net for a homerun.

Feeling the fever and a new brand of confidence, we exploded for 11 runs that inning and went on to win the game handily.

I will never forget that moment. It was the pivotal event of my life. Years prior, I was an obscure, overweight outcast subjected to constant bullying and ridicule. But this event taught me a valuable life lesson; that everyone has a homerun in them as long as you keep swinging for the fence. That's how I've lived my life since that spring day in 1974.

2

Up From the Bootstraps

There comes a time in one's life when inevitability is certain. It could be the prospect of facing one's death or that of a loved one, perhaps a divorce, or that special someone departing for another place. All bring with them a sense of loss.

My first sense of inevitability came in November of 1988. An immense feeling of loss accompanied me when I made the difficult choice to let go of my struggling business and enter into Chapter 7 bankruptcy. I had already turned over my auto-upholstery shop to my future brother-in-law several weeks back. All that was left was my video-appliance store, my pride and joy. I opened Randy's Video-Appliance Store in 1984, when the video rental business was at its peak. Though the store carried my name it wasn't officially mine until July 1986.

I had fallen deeply into debt and further exasperated the problem by trying to keep the store above water by pushing debt beyond the limit; then the Internal Revenue Service and the Arizona Department of Revenue came knocking. My checking account was levied by the IRS and the tax liens began to mount. But I refused to give in. Until the night I wandered into the back room of my store. To this day I cannot recall how it was that I came across this tiny bible of the New Testament. I hadn't seen it since the time it was given to me 10 years earlier when I was in college. I opened the Bible and allowed fate to determine the page that I should read. It opened to Luke 22:39-46.

[39] Jesus went out as usual to the Mount of Olives, and his disciples followed him. [40] On reaching the place, he said to them, "Pray that you will not fall into temptation." [41] He withdrew about a stone's throw beyond them, knelt down and prayed, [42]

"Father, if you are willing, take this cup from me; yet not my will, but yours be done." [43] An angel from heaven appeared to him and strengthened him. [44] And being in anguish, he prayed more earnestly, and his sweat was like drops of blood falling to the ground.

[45] When he rose from prayer and went back to the disciples, he found them asleep, exhausted from sorrow. [46] "Why are you sleeping?" he asked them. "Get up and pray so that you will not fall into temptation."

When I read the passage, it became painfully clear what lay ahead for me. I would close the doors to my store. I understood the road to recovery would be long and treacherous. Yet for the first time, I realized as fully as the situation allowed, the amount of stress and duress Jesus must have felt with the realization of the tribulation that lied ahead for him prior to his crucifixion. His passion gave me strength and the wisdom to understand that, unlike him, I would not walk this road alone.

For the next several years the IRS levied every tax refund to offset back taxes. They also garnished my wages at work. The tax liens by the IRS and the Arizona Department of Revenue were paid in full by 1994.

Approximately ten-years after filing Chapter 7 Bankruptcy, I received an invitation in the mail to apply for a credit card. Due to the bankruptcy, my credit was so bad, as Rodney Dangerfield liked to say, they wouldn't even take my cash. I told my wife Inez that I had applied for the card. She responded, "You know the company you're applying with is very strict don't you? I'm just saying don't feel bad if you get turned down." Several days later, I received a phone call at the school where I worked. They just wanted verification that I worked there. I asked the lady on the other end if I had any chance of being approved. She chuckled and said, "Your chances are pretty good." About a week after the phone call, I received an envelope in the mail. Inside was a shiny new Discover credit card with my name on it. Jumping for joy, I leaped into view of a startled Inez, whipped out the card and proudly declared, "I'm somebody again!" Only in America is such a story possible; where one can lose everything and come back from such a setback, a stronger and better person.

3

The Candidate that came "From the Roots Up"

In early October 2002, I sat pressed in a chair leaning forward resting my arms on a hard table as I took challenging and thought-provoking questions from members of the *Arizona Republic's* editorial board. Flanking me to my right was Republican nominee Trent Franks and to my left Libertarian Edward Carlson. I was the Democratic nominee competing for the congressional seat in Arizona's District 2. It was, by all accounts, a heavily-Republican district.

So much had happened along this journey which brought me to this point. Five months earlier, I was sitting in my backyard porch, sulking. It was my wife Inez's turn to bring out the coffee. She correctly discerned something was wrong. I was turning 42 soon, and had been feeling this increasing sense of urgency since my father's passing four years earlier.

I expressed to Inez that since I was a child, I felt destined for politics. But the road I had traveled had led me elsewhere. In 1978, I was sent off to college with much fanfare from well-wishers only to see myself wither and drop out after a year. Instead, I took a grounds-keeping job at the high school I once attended. What little money I earned went into my midnight-blue 1964 Chevy Impala. On weekends, I would hook up with friends and cruise Central Avenue in downtown Phoenix listening to Oldies and '70s music along the way.

Years later, sitting on the porch assessing my life, I weighed my options. I had already taught high school history for 10 years and absolutely still loved my profession. But the pull toward politics was too much to bear. Inez asked what it was I wanted to do. So I provided her with an answer that was as long as a never-ending novel.

The answer started back in the late spring of 1977 when I sat in a noisy U.S. History class at Tolleson Union High School. My teacher read an announcement about the possibility of one student from our school traveling to Washington D.C. to participate in CloseUp, a one-week program, about how our government functions. He said that the faculty would make the selection and asked if anyone was interested. I raised my hand.

The next day, I was sitting in a study hall playing rummy with my teacher, our reward for finishing work early. I was summoned outside by Mr. Odle, a government teacher, who had come to interview me. He told me I was one of five finalists. The next day, he returned to tell me I was in the final three. The following day, he informed me that I had been selected to represent my school in Washington D.C. I was elated beyond comprehension.

We left on a red-eye flight and arrived in our nation's capital in the early morning, and upon our arrival were subjected to a boring presentation by a state official that put many of us to sleep.

Later, during the week, I had the opportunity to meet freshman Congressman, Bob Stump. I found him a very respectful person. I remember asking him a question during his presentation, which seemed to stump him (no pun intended). I asked, "What have you done to provide help for farm-workers?" He smiled bashfully and then stated, "Honestly, I really can't think of anything at the moment." Though disappointed with his answer, I liked his sincerity.

That trip expanded my interest in politics and in the CloseUp program so much that, 20 years later, I returned as a teacher accompanying my students. Again, Congressman Stump was there to greet us. And it would be this way for several years. Always cordial, he would take us on tours of the Rotunda and to see my favorite statue of Will Rogers. I deeply respected Congressman Stump. His love of country was always paramount. On September 11, 2001, Stump could see the smoke billowing from the Pentagon in the distance. Security was evacuating all congressional offices. Stump ordered his staff to vacate but he refused security officials' order to leave. He remained in his office, steadfast that terrorism would not alter his life or that of his country.

In 2002, Congressman Stump became ill and decided to retire. So there was an open seat available which prompted my interest. What added to my urgency was the fact that the last time this seat was available was when I was in high school some 26 years back.

Uncertainty naturally clouded my view. I had never run or held public office and I realized that a decision to run would likely lead to public ridicule; even among my friends and loved ones. But as Rudyard Kipling said in his poem "If": I had to "make allowances for their doubting too."

Inez suggested that I get myself on the ballot and then decide at that point whether to run. In hindsight, that was not the best idea, because choosing not to run once I'm on the ballot would have validated the doubters' assertions of not taking me seriously. But it sounded like a good idea at the time so I went with it.

I had approximately three weeks to collect nearly 500 valid petition signatures in order to qualify for the ballot in the September primary election, which was only three months away.

It was quite an adventure gathering signatures. I solicited help from friends and family while Victoria, a colleague from work, and I gathered signatures outside a Motor Vehicle Department facility. We had to compete with a paid petition-gatherer who was collecting signatures for various candidates running for different offices. She was earning between $1 and $2 dollars per signature.

She was very unstable and had a short fuse. She would go on to tell us that she was bi-polar. Her erratic behavior posed a tremendous challenge for us. At one point, her and Victoria came to near blows over the subject of abortion. Folks standing in line to renew their car registration and driver's licenses watched in disbelief.

An MVD official warned us that if an altercation happened again, we would be asked to leave and not return. Victoria and I did all we could to avoid her, but as luck would have it, there came another anxious moment.

Violating our agreement, the petition-gatherer stopped sending Independent registered voters over to our table so we stopped sending Independents her way as well. After a while, she started to see how much it was hurting her financially and came after us again. By that point, I had reached my limit with her antics. So, I engaged in a firm conversation with her stating that she had more to lose than me and that I was perfectly willing to go back to our agreement and put this matter behind us. She agreed and was pleasant the rest of the time.

On filing day in early June, I proudly submitted over 550 signatures to the Secretary of State's Office and went home to contemplate a run for Congress.

Several days later, I received a phone call from a surrogate of a congressional candidate named Elizabeth Farley. It seemed she was the odds-on favorite to win the Democratic nomination. She had been campaigning for over a year and had solidified many powerful endorsements including Arizona's AFL-CIO. The reason for the call was to inform me that her campaign believed I had not submitted enough valid signatures to qualify for the ballot and that they were challenging my candidacy. This meant I was going to court. The next day, I received a call from another candidate. Linda Calvert left me a voice message indicating, she too, would be challenging my signatures and taking me to court.

There came a point when I strongly considered dropping out. Then a friend of mine called. When I told him that I was contemplating dropping out, he read me a quote from Teddy Roosevelt:

"It is not the critic who counts; not the man who points out how the strong man stumbles . . . . The credit belongs to the man who is actually in the arena, whose face is marred by dust and sweat and blood; who strives valiantly; who errs, who comes short again and again . . . . and who at the worst, if he fails, at least fails while daring greatly, so that his place shall never be with those cold and timid souls who neither know victory nor defeat."

This quote so greatly inspired me that I decided to fight the challenges. I informed both candidates that if I were not to qualify for the ballot, it would have to be the Secretary of State telling me this, not them.

On July 3, my 42nd birthday, I was in court preparing to hear testimony from Maricopa County's election officials Karen Osborne and Helen Purcell regarding my case.

There were several court cases during that time that provided the courtroom with a carnival-like atmosphere. One centered on a man known as the "sleeping judge." He was in court not as a judge but as a defendant in a competency hearing. He had been diagnosed with narcolepsy, a sleeping disorder where a strong urge to sleep happens at any time. In the case of the sleeping judge, it was while presiding on the bench. Ironically, while seated in the audience directly in front of me during a break in the proceedings, I saw "the sleeping judge" nod off instantly.

Because there were two challenges, it had to be verified by Purcell and Osborne that I had enough valid signatures according to both counts. One count came in at 488 signatures, the exact amount needed. One less and I would have been off the ballot. The second count was just as close; five over.

I wonder how differently my life would have turned out had I not qualified or decided not to run. Would I have been one of those timid souls not knowing victory or defeat Roosevelt referred to that inspired me to press on. My high school basketball coach would to tell me that I played better when I was angry or had something to prove. It was that feeling that moved me in the Spring of 1974 before hitting my homerun.

The petition challenges and time in court angered me. They provoked me to act; being in the state of 'uncomfortable' was a great motivator to fight. Now that I was officially on the ballot, there was no question that I was going to run. Further, when the judge congratulated me and the crowd in the courtroom broke into a raucous cheer, I felt like a candidate. More importantly, the die was cast. I had crossed the Rubicon, the point of no return. I needed a big break to parlay my newfound fortune. It would come the following week. But for the time being, I gathered with family to celebrate my birthday and my decision to run for the United States House of Representatives.

Challenging candidates' signatures is a common practice among politicians because the fewer folks on the ballot the better the chance the remaining ones have of winning. It also knocks the challenged-candidate off balance, dangling in a limbo of legal proceedings rather than shaking voters' hands. For me, the petition challenge took away a vital three weeks of campaigning. As it was, I was entering the election extremely late in the season.

The following week, I took part in an interview with the editorial board of the *Arizona Republic*. When I arrived, I was met by the two candidates that had taken me to court. They were very cordial as we headed up to the interview room in an elevator. There were four Democratic candidates total.

So the members of the editorial board came in and began the interview. Interestingly, this was the first time that The *Arizona Republic* had begun endorsing candidates for office. The interviewers challenged us on various topics. I went into the interview firm in belief that I would tell them everything about me, including what I thought was my biggest weakness, my bankruptcy several years back. When it was over, I replayed the interview in my mind for the rest of the week. I tried hard to be as objective as possible when I evaluated my performance. Unfortunately, there was no one I could ask.

Toward the end of the week, I participated in a candidate forum on the Hopi reservation in the northern part of the state. Victoria once again accompanied me. Being Navajo, she was able to give me valuable insight to the challenges of Native-Americans even the conflict between the Hopi and Navajo.

On our way home, having replayed the *Arizona Republic* interview enough times in my mind, I began to feel confident about the prospect of an endorsement. I'm sure the other candidates believed the same. The following morning, I was awakened by a phone call from a childhood friend crying tears of joy. She had called to tell me that the *Arizona Republic* had endorsed me. It was the break I needed to propel the campaign with credibility.

The endorsement was titled, "Teacher gets Dem nod in Stump's District 2. Our Stand: Camacho, from the roots up."

It was a strong endorsement which read in part, "Camacho brings an impressive up-from-the-bootstraps background, an engaging freshness and a good command of the issues . . . . Camacho demonstrates an understanding of Arizona and the district that can only come from the roots up."

I went on to win a tightly contested primary election besting the second place challenger, Elizabeth Farley, by 513 votes out of 19,709 total votes cast. Several days later, I was officially declared the winner by the Secretary of State's office. I became the Democratic nominee for the General Election. On the Republican side, in a field of seven, Trent Franks emerged as the victor.

Adding to the intrigue was the fact that I had won the primary with about $5,000—as opposed to Farley's nearly $100,000—and what we humorously termed, half a website, because all it contained was a link pointing to the Arizona Republic's endorsement for voters to read. What was once a field of 13 candidates had primarily come down to Trent Franks and political novice Randy Camacho.

As I sat on the hot seat next to Franks, in the second round of interviews with the *Arizona Republic,* there came a point when I had my "Rocky Balboa" moment. It was the point when I felt the separation in our pedigree. Mine was in its infancy. I came from a lineage of proud people that worked the land.

My Grandfather talked of being brought to America in the early '1900s to flee extreme poverty and the Mexican Revolution. Franks came from a family of oil, and as much as many millionaires in politics try to convey that they are self-made; having pedigree and access to others of the same ilk is an advantage very difficult for an opponent, lacking such pedigree, to overcome. It brings to mind the quote, "He was born on third base but thinks he got a triple." No matter how much money I raised, he would raise more. Conversely, nearly half of the members in Congress today are millionaires.

The "Rocky" moment came and went in a blink. I quickly put it away in my mind and focused on the task ahead, to obtain the endorsement and to finish the campaign race strongly. That would be my version of Rocky going the distance; I managed to accomplish both, though, just as in the Rocky movie, the decision at the end of the fight went the other way. Still this experience taught me that there are many good people in America who care about our country. With every speech, with every hand I shook, and with every embrace, I grew as a candidate and as a person validating Tennyson's point in *Ulysses* where he states, "I am a part of all that I have met." From the roots up, is not just the title of an article. It's truly who I am.

ONE

FAMILY AND COMMUNITY

Freedom's promise shines in many ways

"I trust in God, I love my country and will respect its laws. I will play fair, and strive to win; but win or lose, I will always do my best." These are the words to the Little League Pledge we recited in the early '70s after every baseball game.

During the pledge, our hats were placed over our hearts while standing firmly on the foul-line.

Immediately after, we would dash to the concession stand to grab our free snow cone. We thrilled to the sight and sound of clear ice cubes being fed into a grinder that churned out pellets scooped into a paper cone. The ice was so thin it would cave as it retained every drop of the colored flavor that adorned the ice and the taste buds.

My favorite was cherry. Its color matched my uniform. As was customary, the cherry juice would soon alter course running down my hand and forearm, and, like a cat licking its coat, my tongue followed the path of the juice.

Then came the roaring of an onion-hauling truck, faded green in color, as it ground to halt with giant bursts of air blasting through the brakes of its 10 large wheels, signaling to everyone that my ride had arrived. My Brother Ray and I were to stay overnight in a nearby onion field while Leroy and his crew loaded our truck at dawn.

Leroy, a spry African-American man in his early 70s, tossed onion sacks on the back of flatbed trucks with relative ease, singing gospel songs along the way as trucks moved at a sloth's pace. He had a crew of four Black men who were regarded as the best at loading the most sacks—that meant more money—without displacing the weight, which could cause a truck to tip over. This happened one day. There was a truck lying on its side near a canal. It brought to mind the car on the "Flintstones" credits. Loose onions were strewn in every direction. The sacks that remained intact were in a chaotic heap.

After the engines of the lined-up trucks shut down for the night, the only light-source in the truck cab was the rotating beacon of light at Luke Air Force Base. Just a month earlier, while picking onions before the trucking season, I would watch with great pride and fascination as combat aircraft conducted touch-and-goes on the runway. The music playing softly on the radio, in perfect rhythm with the flashing beacon, would lull me to sleep.

It's quite ironic, when one considers, a generally happy little boy in his cherry-stained Little League uniform peacefully lying asleep in an aging truck, without much means but comforted by a beacon of freedom shining proudly in the distance signaling its promise to shine throughout posterity. That's the promise made long ago and its spirit lives in the Little League Pledge.

A tale of three brothers

It's always amazed me how children reared in the same home can wind up with such different characters and personalities. This can be said of my three older brothers; Ruben, the giver, Ray the partier and Ricky, the angry.

Growing up, the four of us shared a small bedroom in a modest home on Pierce Street in the northern part of Tolleson, Arizona. Ruben, the oldest, got the twin bed, Ray and Ricky shared a bunk bed, with Ricky taking the top. Being the youngest, I got stuck with a beige-vinyl couch donated to us by a local elementary school. It came from their teachers' lounge—infested with an ever-present odor of cigarettes. It gave me an eerie feeling, and it didn't help that my brothers constantly joked that it looked like a coffin. At times, on their way to bed, they'd stand at my bedside looking down at me shaking their head with sympathy, as if it were my funeral. They loved giving me a hard time because I had such a bad temper. Sometimes I'd get so angry, I'd throw up.

The corner of the room with the bunk beds where Ricky and Ray slept was a shining example of the different personalities fermenting in our home. Ricky's space was always neat and tidy while Ray's was constantly disheveled. Ricky neatly tacked world maps on his share of the wall while Ray displayed bikini beer models on his.

Of my three brothers, Ruben was the most giving and willing to serve, which is why he joined the United States Army. He also served 25 years in the Army Reserve. In many respects, Ruben was the lion of the brothers. He wasn't tall or muscular but he had a quiet strength about him. There came a time when he landed a salesman job at a Phoenix jewelry store. Ruben did well financially, earning a salary and commission. Having some money empowered Ruben to do the things he'd long desired; like taking me to Phoenix Suns' basketball games when I was a boy. He wanted to expose me to things outside of my limited view of the world. I got to see my favorite players; Dick Van Arsdale and Connie Hawkins take on future legends Jerry West, Wilt Chamberlain and Pistol Pete Maravich.

Ruben also bought me a book by Connie Hawkins called "Foul". I remember one time after a Suns' game; Ruben took me to an area outside of the locker room where players exit on their way to the parking lot. When Connie Hawkins emerged, autograph seekers quickly converged from all directions like a pack of wolves. I stood in the rear of the pack, too small and shy to muscle my way to the front. Suddenly, a giant hand reached across the crowd and snatched the book from my hand returning it quickly with an autograph that read in part, "Peace and Love!" I don't recall if he signed it Connie Hawkins or "The Hawk", but all that mattered was that, for some reason, he noticed me in the crowd of fans. At that moment I felt like I mattered. Ruben's generosity exposed me to experiences that taught me I was not just an observer in this world, I was a part of it. Yet, being a part of this world meant that I had to learn about its people. That's where Ray, the partier, comes in.

Ray was never serious about his education. It took him six years to graduate high school. In fact, Ricky, a couple years younger, caught up to Ray and was already in his second year of college when Ray finally made it out of Tolleson Union High School.

What Ray had going for him though was his charisma. He's a people person. As far back as I can remember, he'd tell me to "always be good to people because you never know when you're going to need their help." And boy was he right. Like the time when the Tolleson community raised over $13,000 in four days to help cover funeral costs when my sister Diane passed away. One major reason for the outpour of support came from the years of personal relationships Ray had established in the community; being there for people in good times and in bad.

People loved to be around Ray. In the mid 70's, he converted a couple of rooms that were attached to the rear of the house, assembled from scraps of an old school building, into a party room. It was lined with Christmas lights that wrapped along the top portion of the walls. Some illuminated beer signs hung on a wall behind a long, dark bar counter that took up a good portion of the party room. Ray's backyard bar—not a real bar—was an instant hit. Folks from the neighborhood brought their own alcohol and would pass the night away playing pool on an uneven billiard table and listening to different kinds of music.

And I was there, hanging out with him every moment. I'd wipe down whatever needed wiping and tossed out the garbage. After each party, Ray and I would go into the kitchen, cook up some breakfast, recount the events of the evening and laugh at the crazy things people did or said at the party. It was more fun hanging out with Ray than it was with my buddies from school. Ray had a unique way of connecting with people. He was a good listener and had a great sense of humor. Whenever I'd ride with him through town, it felt like we were in a parade as folks waved from their front yard or from a passing car. Though Ray wasn't much for school, Ricky, the angry, taught me that education was a ticket to a better life.

Ricky was the middle child. He despised working in the fields, and hated the house we lived in. He'd constantly lash out about how much better others had it, especially when he watched TV commercials. Back then, television was our portal to the rest of the world—and we got to see how well others had it.

There was this television commercial we'd see where a well-dressed homemaker wearing a pearl necklace walked to her round air conditioner thermostat mounted on the wall and turned it counter-clockwise sending a blast of cold air through her warm house bringing quick relief. While this brought a smile to her face, it only served to bring a scowl to Ricky's. Our house was cooled by an old, moldy swamp cooler. Whenever anyone complained that the house was too hot, Ricky went to a nearby wall and mimicked the homemaker in the commercial, turning the knob on a thermostat that didn't exist. Ricky's mocking, which was rooted in anger, always provoked Mom's wrath. She'd say, "Wait until you're older, we'll see just how much better you have it than you do now!"

It was Mom's way of trying to get Ricky to appreciate the things he had, like a roof over his head and food on the table. But that wasn't enough for him. He felt he deserved better.

His anger would also flare as a teen, when he travelled in a rickety old farm workers' bus to a farm field outside of Mesa. He'd stare out the window and see boys his age travelling with their fathers in nice cars. He'd see them heading toward the golf course while his bus turned in the opposite direction onto a nearby lettuce field. His anger and resentment fueled his determination for a better life.

Ricky saw college as an escape, but our family didn't see much value in that path. At least, that's how he tells it. There was one conversation Ricky had with our Tata Teclo, who asked Ricky why he would go to school when there would always be work in the fields. Ricky spat angrily, "I don't want to be flopping in the mud like a pig for the rest of my life!" His words stunned my grandfather. As he took a few steps away from Ricky, he said in a wounded voice: "It's time for me to leave now that I've been called a pig."

It's hard to blame Ricky for his resentment. It was tough enough getting himself through his college coursework, never mind just showing up to class. It was always a crapshoot in his '64 Chevy Impala which often broke down on his 50-minute trek to Arizona State University in Tempe. Ricky stuck with it and earned a bachelor's degree in geography.

Coincidentally, Ricky and I ended up teaching at the same high school, in the same department and across the hallway from each other.

In many ways, I was the fortunate son. Though I spent much of my childhood working in the onion fields, my brothers worked in various types of agriculture throughout high school until they rebelled and found jobs that did not involve toiling on the ground. But what was most fortunate for me was to have three brothers, each with their own set of lenses through which they filtered life.

Taking a piece of each of their lenses—Ruben the giver, Ray the partier, and Ricky the angry—provided me a kaleidoscope of unique perspectives from which to view the world.

The courage of compromise

There have been many memorable debates that I've seen in my lifetime. But the one that stands out most took place between Mom and Dad in the summer of 1970. I was 10 years old at the time. It happened at my Aunt Betty's place in Gilroy, California. She and Uncle Pete brought their family to Gilroy to work the prune orchards. Like many laborers, they were provided temporary housing by the prune grower. Often referred to as campos, the housing units lay in rows like military barracks.

We travelled to California in a 1963 Buick Skylark, absent air-conditioning, to watch my oldest brother Ruben graduate from Army basic training at Fort Ord in Monterrey near Gilroy.

Mom was adamant that Dad stand for the National Anthem at the graduation ceremony. Dad was Jehovah's Witness and Mom a devout Catholic. Following in the footsteps of my Uncle John, Dad converted sometime in the early '1960s. He tried to convert Mom, but she refused as would the rest of us. Jehovah's Witnesses do not vote or take part in the political process because they view it as the stuff of Caesar, not God. It was common practice at the time to remain seated for the National Anthem and the Pledge of Allegiance.

Family members gathered in the small kitchen where Aunt Betty served as moderator. Dad took his podium leaning against a kitchen counter while Mom took hers in the sink area where she washed dishes by hand. The debate commenced with Mom's opening statement. "All these years I've watched you refuse to stand (National Anthem) and I've never said a thing. But I will not watch you do this to your son! We're going to be on a military base. Your son is graduating from the Army! You're going to stand!" Mom lectured Dad. He retaliated, "You're not going to tell me what to do! What I say goes! You hear me?" Then like the Cold War going nuclear, they unleashed a barrage of personal insults from their verbal silos. Dad's refusal had reached its crescendo.

I recall the look of horror on my Grandmother's face. It was painful for her to watch her son battling to maintain authority and the pain of watching a woman defend her son during a time when it was not fashionable to go against the man of the house. Unexpectedly, the debate morphed into a compassionate tone. It touched the human spirit. It was a battle of wills between maternal and paternal instincts. The rambunctious debate ended abruptly as all in attendance quickly exited the kitchen as if they feared the negative atmosphere could be contagious. Dad and Mom made their case with the verdict to be rendered at graduation.

On our way to the ceremony, the anticipation grew like a perfect storm. The moment of truth arrived when a group of soldiers marched in formation to their designated areas; the National Anthem began to play. I peered over toward where Dad was and noticed him respectfully standing. That was surely a sight to behold.

The issue never came up again. Mom and Dad held firm to their belief. Yet during this battle of wills came a moment of clarity; the realization that winning the argument pales in comparison to doing what's right for a son. And if God does not forgive Dad for that, then he is not God.

Patriotism trumps dogma

Sometime in the late '60s, Dad came home after an evening church service anxious to make an 'important' announcement: The world was going to end in 1975. There was no specific date, just that sometime in 1975, it would cease to exist. Being born in 1960, it was easy for me to do the age math. From that point on, I was told to prepare for the end.

During that time, I was in an unenviable position in the family pecking order. Despite his best efforts, Dad could not convert my older siblings, Ruben, Ray, Ricky, and Yolanda from Catholicism to Jehovah's Witness. They had crossed the age threshold and were allowed to decide for themselves. I didn't have that luxury as a child, nor did our youngest sister, Diane. So from fourth grade until the end of my eighth grade year, I endured Kingdom Hall church service and intense bible studies.

Because Dad worked nights as a crane operator for Reynold's Metals Aluminum Plant, Mom ruled the day except Sundays, Dad's day off. As a result, I managed to spend much time at Blessed Sacrament Catholic Church just down the street from my house where I was baptized, confirmed and made my first communion. During Little League season, I would offer flowers to the Virgin Mary prior to our games. Blessed Sacrament is where I felt at home.

But imagine a child growing up with the prospect of the world ending in their lifetime. In one church I was told the end was upon us yet not a mention of it in the other.

Religious conflict posed much stress in our household throughout my childhood. There were the constant arguments between Mom and Dad. He quoted scripture launching attacks on the Catholic Church, while Mom would unleash a salvo of personal attacks until a ceasefire would be declared either by the local police or by a Jehovah's Witness whom Mom trusted would be fair. They were locked in an unrelenting religious conflict mired in dogma that yielded to no one, at times not even the almighty they claimed to worship.

In 1975, America began preparations for its July 4th Bi-Centennial celebration. No one was more interested in the Bi-Centennial than me. Living to see 1976 would mean that the world had not come to an end after all. By this time I was 15 and no longer required to attend kingdom Hall. There was always a side of me that strongly denied the end of the world doctrine, but the thought of it still toyed with me quite a bit.

When New Year's Eve arrived signaling that 1976 was in sight, I anxiously waited for the stroke of midnight. When it arrived, I ran into my Dad's bedroom, shook him awake declaring, "You were wrong!" Dad simply turned away ignoring my gloat.

I don't harbor any ill feelings towards Dad. He meant well. In fact, this experience taught me from a young age what happens around the world does truly matter and that it does have an effect on our daily lives.

When July 4, 1976 rolled around, I felt there was no one happier to be alive and more proud to be an American than me. After all, like our flag giving proof through the night, I was still here.

Death came like a dove—gently and peacefully
(Arizona Republic)

My father and his friend Larry labored tirelessly through the day, tending to pigs and calves at his small ranch in Buckeye when a dove landed on my father's shoulder. It stayed for a moment and then flew away. Larry, a Native American, took special notice. He would share this story continuously. Years later, death came to Dad in much the same way the dove came to him that warm, clear day—slowly, gently and peacefully.

When news anchorman Frank Camacho told his personal story of living with prostate cancer, he made clear the need for prostate cancer awareness. Thankfully, Frank's prognosis is good. The first time I had the pleasure of meeting Frank, he said to me, "So you're the one!" It seems folks would constantly ask us if we were related. No, we aren't.

Though we may not be related, there is a commonality besides our last name. The only difference was the prognosis. When Frank Camacho disclosed his cancer, it was only natural that a flood of memories came to me—of the seven-month journey from the time our father was diagnosed with prostate cancer to the moment he died.

As I prepared for the inevitable, a well-wisher who had recently lost his father to a heart attack stated emphatically that it was better his dad went "quickly" so as not to endure an agonizing wait for his death. Though I cannot speak for him, I will always be grateful for the time I had with my father.

Almost immediately Dad went under hospice care that allowed him to remain at home. I've always felt that the people who work for hospice are angels that walk among us. As the days progressed, Dad suffered immensely from back and leg pain that confined him to a wheelchair. At times, his catheter would become obstructed by the large amounts of cancerous debris. Counting our victories differently by this point, a good day was defined as one where his catheter flowed smoothly and the pain medication was the right dose to keep him as free from pain as possible yet mentally coherent.

He underwent five weeks of radiation treatments at Maryvale Hospital. The doctor promised that at the end of his treatments, Dad would walk out of the hospital without need of his wheelchair. He stressed that the treatments were only meant to give Dad a better quality of life. As promised, on the last day of his treatments, Dad walked out of the hospital.

In the seventh month, awakening from a long sleep, Dad told Mom, "Luz is calling me!" Dad and Grandma Luz always had a special bond. He was her son-in-law, and sadly, she had died the previous year. On July 23, 1998, Dad slipped into a coma. At home, we waited for the end. Manuel A. Camacho died at 12:02 a.m., two minutes into the anniversary of the passing of Grandma Luz.

A nation of profilers

"I've got a couple of free Cardinals tickets. They're yours if you want them." My niece's boyfriend said. I quickly jumped at the chance but it was two hours before kickoff. Who could I get to come with me on such short notice? I settled on a very unlikely choice; my sister Diane. She was reluctant at first but then agreed to come along. Getting Diane to her stadium seat was going to require some tender maneuvering but we were up for the challenge. It had been about seven years since we'd last attended a Cardinals game together.

A rare disease had ravaged her body. It attacked her pulmonary system requiring her to walk around with a unit that pumped medication into the only functioning artery to her heart. An IV tube pierced in her chest pumped medication continuously to keep her artery open. Despite her condition, Diane made every effort to look her best. She wore the latest style clothing and loved name brand purses which she used to store her unit. In fact, at first glance, one would think there was nothing wrong with her. But what this outward appearance wouldn't reveal was that this disease known as, Takayasu's Arteritis, was considered terminal.

The stadium staff and even the fans were incredibly supportive. Fans allowed us to move forward in line while the staff provided us a ride in a cart which took us right up to the entrance. Before we knew it, we were inside the stadium and close to our seats. Diane walked slowly, at times stopping to catch her breath. We discovered the seats were too high. It would be a grueling climb. I noticed a customer service booth and asked if they could assist us. They quickly moved into action escorting us to a disabled section which was lined with folding chairs and sectioned off by rails.

They sat us next to a couple who refused to yield space to make room for us.

It was obvious they were not pleased by our presence. Because they were uncooperative, I was obliged to sit behind Diane. The angry woman asked if we had tickets to sit in that section. Diane explained that she was not able to climb the stairs to her seat so the ushers sat us there. The angry woman replied, "Too many people have been sitting here lately that don't belong here. Our son who's handicapped isn't here today. But we have tickets to sit here."

As the game progressed the angry woman grew increasingly agitated. She fidgeted in her chair, shook her head constantly, and made frequent trips to the snack bar.

I relaxed when the fourth quarter rolled around. I thought the worst was behind us, even when I saw a new usher in our area. But with about seven minutes left in the game the unthinkable happened, the angry woman rose quickly and approached the new usher and marched her over to us. The usher asked to see our tickets.

At that moment, I lost my cool. The angry woman had crossed the line, so I pounced. Ignoring the usher altogether, I moved in front of my sister like a lion protecting its cub and got in the angry woman's face. I screamed through the fan noise, "I can't believe you're still making an issue of this. You're a mean-spirited woman!" Even though she responded with words that were incoherent it was obvious to me that my words affected her. Several ushers from neighboring areas rushed to intervene. The angry woman's husband mumbled some empty threats. It was obvious the angry woman was the dominant of the two.

When the head usher arrived he reiterated we had every right to be there. Fuming, I said, "I don't want to be here with her. It's tough enough what my sister has to deal with on a daily basis and to have to be dealing with this here, especially in this section where, of all people, they (the couple) should understand!"

I could tell these words also had an affect on the woman. But she was committed to acting a fool and her pride would not permit the altering of the course she had embarked upon.

Diane was noticeably hurt by the ordeal but tried to remain positive. Eventually we were moved to another section but by that time the game experience had been ruined. Not even a game-winning field goal could lift our spirits. It's unfortunate that there are people that stoop to the level of profiling others based what they perceive to be a fake disability. Diane's only fault was that she wanted to be like the rest of us, normal. She also wanted to look healthy, and she did. And for that she was chastised because she didn't "look" disabled.

Since then, I have heard many similar stories from folks accused of not being disabled because they didn't look like they were. One involved a teen and her mother who suffered effects from a stroke that caused paralysis on one side of her upper body. When the mom parked in a handicapped parking spot and began exiting her vehicle, she was approached by another woman berating her and saying she should be ashamed of herself for parking in a handicapped spot when it was obvious there was nothing wrong with her.

There is even a website dedicated to reporting people who are parking in handicapped parking spaces who do not 'look' disabled. It asks accusers to provide the placard number of the disabled plate so as to be posted on the website along with a narrative as to why the accuser believes the person isn't disabled. Unfortunately, we've become a nation of profilers, and with every false accusation, the fabric that holds our country together loses a common thread.

Miracle Diane

During my high school years from 1974-1978, Mom was not the person we had grown to know. Her menopausal symptoms were severe. She suffered with its side effects for nearly 10 years until a hysterectomy and periodic hormone shots gave her some relief. But during those tumultuous years prior to her surgery, our family endured a great deal of emotional stress which tested our character and resolve.

I missed seeing Mom in the stands at my basketball games after she had faithfully attended every game during my freshman year. Without warning she stopped coming. She could not be around people. Dad did the grocery shopping. When I spoke at my graduation ceremony, Mom listened to my speech from a nearby baseball field where Dad had laid a blanket on the outfield grass for Mom to sit on.

Suffering from hot flashes, Mom would sit in front of the swamp cooler letting the cool air blast over her body while fanning herself with whatever paper product she could find. Yet, a heating pad rested on the back of her neck. Then there were the mood swings which would erupt like Vesuvius, sending me and my siblings scattering in different directions.

Dad worked the graveyard shift. When I would come home from school, he would be asleep. Then, Dad would wake up while we were in bed. We could hear his utensils clanging softy in the kitchen as he ate his midnight meal before heading to work.

Then, like clockwork; the sound of Dad revving the engine of his morocco-brown pickup would follow. (It would warm up on the way to the plant.) As the sounds of the pickup faded into the midnight silence, there would be one more toss and turn in our beds as we free-fell to sleep with the returning calm of the night.

Like the recurring scene in Ground Hog Day, the chaos of Mom's menopausal symptoms would return at sunrise when she woke up. The combination of Mom's menopause and the religious tension between her and Dad caused us to retreat into ourselves to escape the chaos. There came a point where we started living our own separate lives within our house. Many times, I prepared my own meals which got me to enjoy cooking.

My sisters Yolanda and Diane took over many of Mom's duties. Yolanda did much of the cooking. Diane would wait up for me when I was away at a basketball game. When I arrived, she would prepare a meal consisting of a sandwich, chips and milk.

She listened intently as I gave her the play by play accounts of the game.

I have always felt that in many ways, I raised Diane. She was the youngest of the family; three years my junior. Several years after I graduated high school, I returned to my old stomping grounds to watch Diane play basketball. She was quite an athlete. Her coach was so impressed with her character that he decided to pay our family a visit to express those thoughts personally.

Shorty, after my Dad's passing in 1998, Diane became pregnant with her second child. There came a point in her pregnancy where things started to go wrong. Shortly after, we were summoned to the hospital where we were told she had lost her baby. I sat close to her in the hospital room offering whatever I could in way of support. She was visibly depressed over the loss of her baby.

Adding to our concern, Diane gave us some disturbing news. She said, "I've got something else to share with you, the doctor says they've discovered a heart murmur and now they want to run more tests on me." A nurse allowed me to listen to the murmur with her stethoscope. I heard a swooshing sound where there should have been a heartbeat.

Later, Diane would be diagnosed with a rare disease called Takayasu's Arteritis, also called the "pulseless" disease. It strikes one in 2 million, mostly women and people of Asian ancestry. It is an autoimmune disease that strikes the arterial circulation of the body causing arteries to inflame inflicting severe damage by affecting or stopping blood flow in certain parts of the body. In Diane's case, it struck in her pulmonary and heart system. Blood flow to her right lung was completely cut off reducing Diane to function on one lung whose artery was always in danger of closing.

We took several trips to California for various procedures, including a long open-heart surgery. Despite reassurances from us that folks lived long lives with this disease, there was no getting around the fact that the life expectancy of someone with Takayasu's Arteritis is about ten years. Knowing this, Diane prayed to God to grant her enough life to watch her son LJ graduate from high school. Her prayers were answered when she attended his graduation ceremony in the spring of 2009.

In September 2009, I received a call at work that Diane had just a few hours to live. We gathered at the hospital and prepared for the end. We met with the doctor and were told that her organs were shutting down. It hurt me to do this but when I went in to see Diane, I whispered in her ear that it was okay to let go. She retorted "No, No, No, don't say that!"

St. Joseph's, a Catholic hospital, contains a beautiful church. I suggested to my family that we attend the evening service. It was an inspiring mass. I don't recall ever praying so hard. I prayed that no matter the outcome, for God to take care of Diane.

The following morning, Doctors called us in to inform us that the worst was over. Surprisingly, her organs had made a comeback and her vitals had stabilized. She had come storming back from the abyss. Shocked at the outcome, doctors nicknamed her "Miracle Diane."

When I returned to visit her, I felt embarrassed that I had even suggested for Diane to let go. We never spoke of it. But I made it a point not to suggest that again no matter how dire things might appear. I sat on her bed, as I always did, rubbing her feet, which likely brought me more comfort than her.

Tired but inspired, she told me that something incredible had happened during the night when she was left in fate's hands. She recalled how the nurse turned off the lights to her room. It was the same nurse that told Diane she had about 24 hours to live. Diane told me that sometime during the night, "The room suddenly lit up! But it wasn't the same type of light that would come from the ceiling. I knew it was different." She went on to say, "At that moment, I felt everyone's prayers and I felt the presence of all the saints. Next thing I know I heard the doctor's voice calling to me and saying I had made it past the danger point, which is when I heard him call me 'Miracle Diane'."

Diane would live for another year. Her 11-year battle came to an end on August 17, 2010, when the stint in her left pulmonary artery penetrated her airway causing internal bleeding. Her passing brought our community together as they rallied in support of our family. Diane worked at a local doctor's office for more than 20 years. Always cordial, she was a person well-loved in our community. I miss her dearly.

Diane had a special saying for everyone who she was parting way with—A goodbye wasn't acceptable; instead, she always said: "Don't say goodbye. Say, see you later!" I look forward to that day.

TWO

TREASURED MEMORIES

Canals evoke memories of a simpler time

As I rode on my uncle's back, he gazed anxiously at the stream below, looking for a good spot to dive in. When he found the perfect place, he told me to hold my breath and hang on tight. Suddenly a rush of cold water penetrated my nose and ears but I did not let go. I knew better. I was just a child at the time; letting go could have meant my life.

In the distance, family members placed blankets on the hood of their cars. Massive pecan trees provided shade. As they enjoyed food and drinks, they talked and laughed while listening to music blaring from a car radio. All this before they, too, would take a cool plunge in the water.

I felt safe that day riding on my uncle's back as he dog paddled along the large canal near 91st Avenue and McDowell. Paying little heed to the notion that I was not a gifted swimmer, I grew up splashing in many of the Valley's canals and *pompas* (watering holes) where families gathered for adventure and relaxation during a much simpler time when the grass seemed greener and the sun less searing.

Talk to anyone who grew up with this experience and their stories begin to flow with a strong current of memories just as clear as the flowing canals that have brought life to the Valley since the days of the Hohokam. "I remember riding on inner tubes in the late '60s south of Van Buren and 91st Avenue until eventually the canal was covered up," Henry Bustamante recalls.

In the evening, there was the famed "Dixie Bubbles," a favorite hangout near 99th avenue and McDowell Road, where party-goers would swing from a tire swing before plunging into the canal. Yet, just as the flowing canals brought life to the Valley, their unforgiving currents have also brought tragedy. There have been a considerable amount of drownings over the years. Some as a result of swimming accidents while others a result of vehicle accidents.

One memorable occurrence was when a young adult female dove into a large canal with her husband but never surfaced. The surrounding communities searched for her body. In a morbid scene, the townspeople brought refreshments and food in anticipation of a long day of searching. Just as in the movie *Stand by Me*, we embarked on a journey to locate a corpse. And like Huckleberry Finn, as we journeyed on foot along the water's path, our travels opened my eyes to places I had yet seen as a young boy.

It would stand to reason that some readers might have difficulty relating to this story, believing it to be a set of isolated incidents that affected a handful of people native to this area. Yet, the canals of the Valley, in one form or another, have touched souls from all walks of life. And as they continue to flow, so do the fond memories of a much simpler time.

Family memories released in aroma of soup

In December of 2007, I took it upon myself to learn how to make menudo, a spicy Mexican soup consisting of beef tripe and hominy. The long, arduous process would require about six hours. Growing up, I had seen Mom and Dad prepare the concoction in a large pot that would take up two burners on our gas stove. There were also times where my dad prepared menudo outdoors over a fire. From start to finish, the production of menudo was always an eventful experience in our household.

The six-hour journey would take place on my gas grill in my backyard with a pot less than half the size my parents used to cook on. Once the soup began simmering, the aroma emanating from the various spices tantalized my mind to the extent that I began to remember the past with all my senses. I could even smell it. Memories long stored in my mind's hard drive downloaded suddenly, opening up a Web page of memories clear and distinct. With each step completed in the soup-making process the memories boiled into every fabric of my senses.

With great clarity, I recalled how my grandfather would plant a garden in the backyard of each home belonging to his sons. He would enter from the alley sporting a wheel barrel, hoe and shovel. Of course, I would assist him. Each backyard was home to different crops. Ours happened to be a garlic and cilantro garden, two important spices for preparing menudo.

When relatives would make menudo they would come to our garden to pick the garlic and cilantro. They would leave, taking with them one of our small pots. It would inevitably be delivered to us at suppertime—filled to the brim with the hot steaming soup.

When my journey was complete, what stood before me was not just a spicy soup, it was history dating to the days in Mexico where the rich landowners would keep the best meats of the cow and the peasants were left to their creative talents to make use of all the leftover parts given to them. I had learned to make something special and unique.

With the announcement that the menudo was ready, family members converged on our home. Menudo brought us together that cold December day as it has always done in times past. Interestingly, as they ate, they shared stories long forgotten. For a precious moment they clung to those old tender years.

Then it dawned on me. Maybe it's the spirit of our loved ones from the past that resides in our favorite foods. Or perhaps it's our senses coming to life with every aroma from a time long forgotten; senses we have suppressed in favor of life's daily routine, which can lull us into a melancholy madness.

The making of menudo taught me one valuable lesson. If you want to remember the past with all of your senses, recall that special dish that was the staple of your family and start cooking.

THREE

A DIFFERENT SET OF LENSES

Cope by putting life events in perspective

During an unseasonably hot spring day in 1980, a young teen named Tacho played joyfully on a 10-ton tractor as his family of siblings and cousins napped comfortably while taking a break from work at a nearby cotton field.

His 10-year-old cousin Gordo, 14-year-old cousin Rachel and Grandmother rested in the shade as well. The family was unaware that Tacho was in the cockpit of the tractor play steering. The enormous scoop of the tractor was in a stationary position trumpeting silently into the sky while providing shade for the family below.

Tacho began to play with the levers. He pulled a lever that brought the massive scoop storming down toward the unsuspecting family below. Alerted, they scattered to escape the giant steel beast crashing upon them. All managed to escape except for Gordo, Rachel and their grandmother. The family frantically dug and clawed in a desperate but feeble attempt to free them. The more they dug, the more the unforgiving scoop pressed its victims into the earth. Tacho would lose both cousins and grandmother that fateful day, causing him to withdraw from the world.

Several months later, I was assigned by the school that employed me as a high school dropout recruiter to visit Tacho in hopes of convincing him to return to school. As I became familiar with his story, I thought to myself: "What am I going to say when I meet Tacho for the first time?"

Since the accident, Tacho slept throughout the day, spoke on rare occasions and would wait for his family to leave the dinner table before sitting down for dinner alone.

After a long day of prodding, his family and I were able to convince Tacho to return to school. He would first meet with the school psychologist, who I asked, "What could you possibly say to this young man that would make him want to go on with his life?"

He smiled and said he told Tacho it took many events to make this accident occur. First, there was the cotton field that brought the family there to work, the unseasonably hot day prompting the family to seek shelter beneath the tractor, the tractor driver who left the scoop up instead of locking it into the ground, and the family's decision to rest beneath the tractor.

He pointed to other events both large and small that played a role in the accident. According to the psychologist, Tacho pulling the lever, however severe, was one factor in a larger set of factors.

Tacho stayed in school for a short time and dropped out once again. Word came that he had joined his relatives working in construction and had become part of the family once more. I would never see Tacho again. But I will always remember the smile on his face as he exited our office after gaining a new perspective of a tragic event.

Surely, there are many walking among us today who carry a heavy burden, perhaps even guilt over a dreadful experience from the past that continues to haunt them on a daily basis. Perhaps, Tacho's story will shine a new light of perspective in a place we call life.

Stop and gain perspective

In 1982, I took a job that, in retrospect, may have been too young to have. I was 22 at the time, when I became a maintenance supervisor at a local elementary school. I oversaw a budget of about three-hundred-thousand dollars and a crew of about 12 employees consisting of groundskeepers, custodians and an overzealous maintenance worker named Tony.

By all accounts, it was a stressful job riddled with school politics. Being young and inexperienced made it difficult to gain respect among my much older employees, especially one who happened to by my uncle. Who could blame him; he was our supervisor when we worked in the fields. Tom, our superintendent and my boss, was well aware of the landscape that posed much duress among the employees in my department, including myself.

Tony was a talented maintenance man; versatile in his trade. Though he and I got off to a good start initially, there came a point in our working relationship where things began to sour. Tom became aware of the problem. Fearing I was about to let Tony go, he assigned him to a special project, placing him directly under Tom's supervision. I felt somewhat betrayed but understood Tom's desire to secure Tony's talents. Quite often, word would come to me that Tony was gunning for my job and working directly with Tom was the first step in the process.

I continued to learn my job on the fly. One point of contention among my crew was the weekly meetings I held with them on Mondays. They felt I was taking them away from their duties and,

Tony being excused from these meetings, further exasperated the problem.

There was little doubt that Tony was taking great delight with my slow descent into hot quicksand as I struggled to maintain stability in my department. The bickering among my staff grew exponentially. Nothing I tried seemed to work. Through it all, I wondered what 'special' project Tom had Tony working on.

The hub of our school district lay in a former bank building we called the District Office. It was home to various departments. Walking down the hallway, one would catch a glimpse of the vault the bank used long ago. Tom disliked seeing the vault on a daily basis. He felt its presence gave our office the feel of the old bank and not of a contemporary district office.

So he assigned Tony the task of removing the vault. Measurements were taken, weight was approximated, and various consultants were brought in to assess the conditions and to offer recommendations. The vault was the size of a small room. Encased in heavy-duty steel, it was extremely heavy and virtually impenetrable by most means; which was what it was designed to do.

After much deliberation, Tom and Tony decided to employ a demolition company that was going to use dynamite to separate the vault from the building structure, and then heavy machinery would tow the vault away from the building. Afterward, Tony would repair damage done to the building.

On the day of an upcoming board meeting, I was summoned to Tom's office. "Randy, out of courtesy, I want to provide you with the plans—including various blueprints—for the vault removal before presenting them to the school board at tonight's meeting," he said as he shuffled through piles of paper work on his desk. Tom was likely being proactive because in all likelihood, I was going to be asked to comment on the plan. Tony was present as Tom explained the ambitious plan which was going to cost more than $5,000.

When Tom was done, I looked at both of them—with a poker face expression of a card player not wanting to reveal their hand—then presented Tom with a simple question. "What's the main issue with the vault?" I asked. "It makes our office resemble a bank." Tom replied. I asked, "In what way?" Exasperated he said, "Look Randy, the deposit drop-box connected to the vault on the outside of the building gives it that look! Okay?" The deposit drop box, which resembled an ATM, and the vault were one of the same. It was used by nighttime merchants who would deposit their money during non-bank hours. They would open the trap door which would open toward the person just enough to slide the deposit bag through. Once the trap door was closed, it would become part of the wall again. So the appearance of the bank is on the outside of the building, not the inside, I quickly surmised.

I asked to see the plans again. Looking at the drop box and the building's proximity to a busy crosswalk where many folks would congregate, gave me an idea. "I have an idea. Just hear me out! Let's purchase four 2"X6" boards, a piece of plywood and a sheet of cork-board." I went on to say, "With these materials we'll construct a bulletin board the community can use. We'll attach it to the building and cover the drop box simultaneously."

There was a long awkward pause. Dumbfounded, Tom quickly removed his cigar from his mouth; Tony smiled shyly, like when the dealer calls, "Craps!" What was shaping to be a monumental project that included the use of dynamite, demolition, and major renovation to the building and would've cost several thousand dollars was easily resolved for less than $20. Ironically, Tony was assigned the task of constructing the bulletin board.

Consider why Tom and Tony were not able to see this obvious solution. Tom's assumption was that the vault needed to be removed. Where Tony failed was in not stepping back and asking the right questions. Perhaps his desire for my job clouded his judgment.

A story I heard recently reminded me of the vault incident. It's about a little boy who went for a walk with his grandfather. The little boy pointed to different things as they walked asking what each was. When the boy pointed to a road sign the grandfather said, "That's a stop sign. Whenever you see it, stop, look around and see all the beautiful things around you." Ironically, the same can be said of life, a stressful job, or taking on a special project. I'm reminded of this every time I think back to the vault or happen upon a stop sign on a morning walk.

FOUR

THE WONDER OF FAITH

Despite tragedy, faith guides retiring deacon

Decades ago, in present day Sun City, a young Tony Chavez bounced gingerly on a tractor as he plowed rows of field in preparation for the cotton season. It was important to keep the rows straight, so Tony would use the radiator cap at the front of the tractor to guide him. At times, he'd give in to uncertainty and would look back to make sure the rows he had plowed were straight. But, every time he looked forward again he had veered off course. As he matured, he learned to trust his faith and not look back at what he had plowed. Little would he realize how much this simple lesson in faith would prepare him for the biggest test of his life.

In the fall of 1973, Tony's 10-year-old daughter, Regina, walked to school as most children routinely did in the small Tolleson community. Along the way, she'd pass the Blessed Sacrament Church. As she continued on, Regina would see neighbors standing in their front yard watering the grass and chatting about the day's events. Nearing the school, Regina would follow a chain-link fence about two blocks before entering the school grounds. This day, however, would be different than most. Regina noticed that her pet dog had followed her to school. As she headed home to return her dog, school went into session. And for an unforgiving moment in time, the town slept and Regina vanished. She had been abducted.

Having lost its innocence, the entire community was shaken to its core. Sidewalks and streets were void of playing children. Parents scrambled to drop their children off at school and to pick them up at the end of the day. Local and national media coverage was at a fever pitch. A photo of Regina in her first-communion dress and Tony's pleas for her safe return blanketed the airwaves. Some time later, Tony's worst nightmare would come to pass. Regina's body was discovered in a nearby cotton field. The perpetrator, a man from Indiana who happened to be passing through Tolleson, was eventually caught and convicted.

One could conclude that it would be natural for Tony to take this tragedy and turn to a life of hatred and anger. Instead, like the cotton fields he had plowed, Tony cultivated his faith and refused to look back. Several years after Regina's death, Tony became a deacon for Blessed Sacrament Church. He has served its parishioners honorably for 30 years.

Slowed by time and fate, the deacon will be retiring soon. To honor him, the community recently held a banquet to celebrate and to show its gratitude one final time. I suspect an even bigger banquet awaits Deacon Tony Chavez in the future.

Wrestler's faith prepares coach for end

Sweating profusely, high school senior Robert Fisher III padded himself down with a drenched towel. This would be his final practice; the 1997 Wrestling State Tournament had arrived. Clamoring for a sense of Robert's confidence Westview Head Wrestling Coach Mick Barone asked Robert if he was ready. Fisher's response was not one the coach expected.

"I'm not worried Coach, I'm gonna take it all because God and I have an agreement" he declared. Barone was not a person of great faith. His positive response came halfhearted at best. Fisher went on to explain how he had emerged from a "deep prayer" in which he had promised God that if he would win the state tournament he would not attend a university but would instead enroll in a seminary to become an ordained minister. He went on to tell coach Barone that "God agreed" so long as Fisher kept his end of the bargain and prepared himself to the best of his ability. This is what he had been doing the entire season. Pushing himself beyond the limits during practice; even running five miles every evening.

This was the first year that the 215 pound weight class had been added by the Arizona Interscholastic Association. "Formally in the 189 weight class, 215 was a perfect fit for me. Also, it just so happened that my first hour class was weightlifting and that really helped my strength and stamina, everything seemed to be in place."

Unfortunately, Fisher drew the most difficult wrestling bracket. He was familiar with every wrestler in this bracket because he had wrestled each one during the regular season; one being a returning state champion. "I'm not worried Coach, I'm gonna take it all." Fisher continued to proclaim to a nervous Coach Barone.

As Fisher continued to advance in the state tournament he would seek out Coach Barone after each victory "I'm telling you coach I'm gonna take it all." In the semi-final he would face the defending state champ. He would win in overtime but suffered a critical ankle injury. "I honestly believe that I won that match because I was able to outlast him," Fisher said. But Fisher's ankle was in a bad state. His mother tried to convince him not to continue; Fisher asked the trainer to tape his ankle tighter to see if it would hold. It did. So he continued. He would go on to win the state title; Winning every match in overtime. Fisher fulfilled his promise to become an ordained minister and continues to serve today.

Coach Barone often expressed the profound effect this event had on his life. Sadly, a few months after the state tournament, Coach Barone was diagnosed with terminal colon cancer. And it would be fitting that the coach known for his wit, humor and practical jokes would pass away on April Fools Day in 1999. He was 39.

Of his former coach Fisher says "I wanted to be a positive footnote in his life." Perhaps Fisher's journey of faith was in the end destined for Coach Mick Barone; to prepare him for what was to come.

FIVE

LEARNING MOMENTS

History lesson invokes uneasy feelings in class
Part I

The year was 1988, and Tom had just purchased an auto-upholstery shop in the Valley. He hired David, an experienced upholstery trimmer, who had previously worked at the shop and knew many of the customers. Tom was new to this type of business. He purchased the shop in hopes of keeping another business, a flailing video-appliance store, afloat.

As a point of fun, David informed Tom that upon removing car seats for upholstering, they would often find loose change on the floor beneath. David also mentioned that it was tradition to gather the loose change and place it into a coffee can, and by weeks end, there would be enough change to pay for breakfast. Tom paid little thought to the tradition and did not stand in its way.

But one day, a customer brought in a pickup truck to have its seat upholstered and indicated he would pick up his vehicle at the end of the day. Tom and David playfully raced as they removed the bolts securing the seat to the floor. Once the seat was removed, they jumped into the truck. Like kids in a playground they laughed as they picked coins off the carpet.

Then, David noticed two small slits in the carpet, which appeared to have been made by a sharp object, perhaps a razor. David peeled back the piece of carpet and pulled out a wad of money. Crisp and new, the money totaled $640. So, if you were Tom what would you do with the money? This was the question I posed to my World History class one day as an administrator performing an annual evaluation looked on. To add to the scenario, I indicated to the class that if they chose to keep the money, the customer would never know.

The class was divided into two groups. On one side were students who said they would take the money. On the other side were those who said they would return the money. The groups faced off. I moderated the loud and heated debate in a class where students choosing to keep the money were in the majority. Feeling that many of their friends could no longer be trusted, some students became extremely emotional. The debate also had an effect on the administrator. He got up, shook his head and left. Remember, this was a debate that required honesty. The students choosing to keep the money were simply being honest. Some reasoned that it was the customer's fault for leaving the money in the truck. Others felt the students who advocated returning the money were not truly being honest; that in a real situation they would take the money.

This scenario struck a chord with my students. As for the administrator, he would later confirm that the lesson weighed heavily on him for quite some time.

Had the administrator stayed a bit longer, he would have learned that the Tom and David story was for the most part true except for one detail: I was Tom. Stay tuned for the longest day of my life.

Let moral compass not others guide your principles
Part II

I got out of the truck we were set to upholster with $640, found beneath the floor carpet. I began dialing the phone to contact the customer. David, an employee, followed me into the office saying, "What are you doing? You know you need the money. Both your businesses aren't doing well. This money will help you."

Unfortunately, I was unable to reach the customer and it would be that way the rest of the day. David meant well. He knew my video-appliance store and upholstery shop were on the brink of extinction. My inability to reach the customer and David's overzealous desire to help created a perfect storm that would test my ability to stand against a raging tide of opinion.

David summoned every person he could think of in hopes of convincing me to change my mind. One person of faith rationalized that perhaps God had placed the money there for me. With news traveling quickly through my family circle, my aunt, whom I hadn't spoken to in years, called and chastised me, saying, "If he was stupid enough to leave the money in the truck, then he deserves to have it taken!" People I loved and respected, who had taught me right from wrong, strongly urged me to see it their way. I felt their will pressing upon me to do something I knew was wrong. I understood that by going against the wishes of those I admired, I was going to look like a *fool*.

It brought to mind George Orwell's *Shooting an Elephant*, in which a British police officer in Burma pursued an elephant that had gone on a rampage after escaping its owner. It had killed a person. When the officer came upon the elephant, it was no longer angry and was feeding peacefully on some grass in a nearby field. The officer had no desire to shoot the animal, but soon felt the will of several thousand Burmans pressing upon him to shoot the elephant. He shot the elephant only so as not to look like a fool.

Our customer picked up his truck and left. David, who was under strict orders to call me when the truck's owner arrived, didn't mention the $640. "You'll see," David said. "He'll never know!"

That evening, I returned the money to the customer and his stunned wife. He smiled while quoting the exact amount. He had been looking for the money for some time and had given up hope of finding it. The next day, I told David about a new policy. Whatever change was found underneath a car seat would go to the customer at the end of the day.

Eventually, I would lose both businesses. Looking back to that long, trying day, I think of those who wanted me to keep money that did not belong to me. I also consider how different our world would be if we allowed folks to make decisions based on their moral compass rather than others. Twenty years ago, I chose not to shoot the elephant, and to this day in the eyes of many, I was a fool.

One person's generosity makes another ponder right reaction

Recently, while tending to my monthly fix of Chick-Fil-A, I patiently navigated the crowded drive-through. After placing my order, I scrounged around the ashtray in hopes of collecting the exact change. As I looked ahead, I noticed a red pickup truck. It was neither new nor old. The reason I say "noticed" is because there was something about the truck that caught my attention. I can't tell you why; just call it instinct. On the rear was a bumper sticker that read, "Army Rangers . . . Only Send the Best."

Receiving his order, the gentleman in the red pickup truck drove off. A Chick-Fil-A employee stood with my order while waiting for my car to dock with her window. After a successful docking, she handed me my order and proceeded with an announcement that sounded more like a prepared statement. She said, "Sir, I just want to let you know that your order has been paid for by that gentleman in the red truck." Dumfounded, I said, "Really?" She smiled and said, "Yeah, he does it all the time. He pays for the order of the person behind him every time he comes through." So I opened my ashtray, re-deposited my loose change and drove away with a newfound perception of the old adage: "left holding the bag."

I decided to share my story with colleagues at work. While most were really touched by the act, I was quite surprised when one person in the room said, "That would have ticked me off if a complete stranger would've paid for my order like that. I don't ask anyone for help. I find it offensive." I was taken back by his point of view because it had never occurred to me that doing a good deed—like buying someone a meal—might be deemed offensive by the recipient. Of course, he was in the minority.

Perhaps this is why the gentleman in the red truck does this, to make us see our world a little differently. But it does bring to mind this question: How should I react to such an act of kindness? Do I simply appreciate the gesture and move on? Or do I return the act of kindness by purchasing someone else's meal the next time I'm at a drive-through? Or like my colleague at work, should I have been angry and found the act offensive? Perhaps I'm reading too much into this.

I've decided how I'm going to respond to this generous act, but like the blank screen on the *Sopranos* final episode, I will leave the ending to you. So how will you respond should you come across the gentleman in the red truck and he picks up your tab?

Life's learning moments precious, must be seized

One day, I was taking a walk on campus at the high school where I teach when overhead appeared a large flock of geese in a V-formation. In the distance a group of students watched, with great fascination, as the noisy flock flew by. Sensing a learning moment, I approached the group and asked, "Do you know why birds, such as geese, fly in a V-formation? Because the bird at the front softens the head wind and causes less resistance for the others. Then they switch when the lead bird gets tired. That's why they're able to travel long distances."

Truth be told, every moment we live is a learning moment. In the case of the students, I was learning how to teach them something new as they learned about the flying habits of birds. There is a life application to birds flying in a V-formation. For example, a good leader takes on the headwinds of resistance. The role and competence of the leader is vital to the survival of the flock. By taking on the headwinds, the leader makes the function of the others much easier, allowing for learning moments to flourish.

It is believed that the lead bird flies at a slightly different altitude to allow the rest to clearly see the path ahead and when they are upon their target. In much the same way, a good leader creates a vision that stakeholders buy into and follow, working in tandem to reach their destination. When the lead bird is ready, it drops back to the rear of the flock allowing others to take the lead. In much the same way, a good leader sets the parameters and expectations and then empowers others to carry out their responsibilities.

In many respects, today's schools are in a perpetual state of learning moments that are not exclusive to the classroom. An administrator in charge of student discipline said even though her job was to punish students who had broken a rule, she would make it a point to teach students what they had done wrong and attempt to counsel them into changing their negative behavior into a positive one.

Unfortunately, with today's political vitriol, in-your-face TV reality shows, trash-talking athletes, attention-seeking scoundrels and the endless demands life places upon folks in general, it's sometimes difficult to notice the learning moments when they present themselves. When this happens, we lose an incredible opportunity to advance ourselves and our society. Which is why learning moments are like birds of a feather that really do flock together. And when they appear, as it did for me and a group of students, it is important to seize the learning moment before it flies away.

SIX

INSPIRATIONAL STORIES

Old wrestler revives dream of competing

Staff members at Ira Murphy Elementary School in Peoria noticed the gradual weight loss of Assistant Principal Sammy Chagolla. His friends and family had observed the physical change, as well. Sammy's ill-fitting clothes were beginning to hang from his shrinking body. But, no one could build up the nerve to ask the simple question, "Sammy, are you all right? Are you dying?"

For Sammy, the story begins in July 2008, when his wife, Carrie, gave him a letter she happened upon while both were looking through some old wrestling photos. Sammy had written the letter to himself in 1988 at age 23, after he failed to make the U.S. Olympic wrestling team. The letter was full of regret and second-guessing. He believed he should've wrestled in a lower weight class. He also believed he had let his coach, family and teammates down. This sinking feeling of a dream unfulfilled prompted Sammy to write the letter.

Sammy wrote, "If I'm healthy at the age of 45, I will train to wrestle in a big national wrestling tournament. Maybe if I'm healthy and daring, I can just enjoy the battle of the sport of wrestling. I don't know if this will happen, but I'm a dreamer . . . . I hope God will help me get past the failure of the Olympic

Trials." He also promised to become a wrestling coach for Peoria and guide them to a state championship; which he did.

So that evening, Sammy located his old jogging shoes and began training privately. For months Sammy concealed from everyone the dream that had thrust itself upon him. He's a private person and didn't want the added pressure. By November, Sammy had shed nearly 40 pounds. He was weighing in at 138, one weight class lower than the weight he wrestled at in the Olympic Trials. Interestingly, Sammy lost the weight naturally by eating and training properly, a far cry from his training method 20 years earlier, which consisted of starving himself to make weight. Looking back, had he trained this way and wrestled in a lower weight class it might have made the difference in making the Olympic team.

Sammy would go public with the wrestling news in April. But not before he was on his way to Las Vegas to take part in the Veteran's National Championships in an effort to undo 20 years of regret. It meant a great deal to Sammy to have his former high school coach in his corner. Sammy would go on to place second in the 138.5 weight class, ages 40-48. Greatly elated, Sammy felt a tremendous weight lifted from his shoulders.

Sammy's journey was supposed to end in Las Vegas. But, placing second in the national tournament qualified him to participate in the World Championship Tournament in Turkey in August. Sammy is wrestling with raising $5,000 to cover the cost of the trip. The "Little Wrestler Who Could" has proved he has one more in him and his arduous long journey serves as an inspiration to all who believe they have one more in them, as well.

Here's to celebrating non-traditional views

The annual Whoopee Daze Parade is a Tolleson tradition that goes back as long as I can remember. Held in May, it features the same pomp and circumstance of all parades—decorated horses, vintage cars, marching bands and since elections have come and gone, maybe an occasional waving politician. Organizers will also tussle with the decision on who to select as the grand marshal, and I would like to make the selection process a little easier for the committee by recommending a nominee. I'm sure there are many candidates well deserving of this honor. But none more than Archie.

Archie doesn't have a last name but he does have a title: the *World's Ugliest Dog*. Archie is a hairless Chinese crested with four teeth, a hanging tongue, and little hair; except for the few strands sticking up like a pincushion on top of his head. In an unconventional way, Archie, who resides in Tolleson, has turned our perception of ugly into quite a beautiful story.

No, this is not a joke or an effort to disparage the title of Whoopee Daze grand marshal, but an honest attempt to compel committee members to take Archie's nomination idea to heart and to chew on it a little.

What can one say of Archie who two years ago was in animal shelter moments away from being put to sleep? He was unwanted in this dog-eat-dog world. As the final hours ticked away, Archie's life flashed before his eyes. Fate intervened when he was adopted by Heather Peoples, who was practically paid by employees at the shelter to take the pooch.

Approximately a year later, after being prodded by a friend, Peoples traveled to Petaluma, Calif., and entered Archie in the World's Ugliest Dog contest. Archie was an obvious underdog. The competition was fierce but Archie won over the judges and the crowd when he was rolled onto his back exposing his mole-peppered stomach, prompting the crowd to chant: "Archie, Archie, Archie!"

In overcoming the odds, Archie has touched the human spirit and has proved that everyone, no matter what status in life, serves a purpose and should not be taken for granted. Our world has become easily accustomed to acting only positively toward superficial features we deem to be acceptable and coldly rejecting those who tend to be different. Archie was but a mere example of this practice. And this practice nearly cost him his life.

If parade organizers should decide to choose someone else to be grand marshal of the upcoming Whoopee Daze Parade, at the very least we can declare Archie our grand marshal as we parade through life.

Tolleson's new vice mayor lives life by the moment

The first day of school in August of 2001 began normally for 26-year-old kindergarten teacher Anna Tovar. She watched joyfully as nervous and happy children filed into her classroom clutching a grown-up's hand. Though Anna was feeling a bit sluggish, she dismissed it as getting used to the school routine again. Several days later, strange red dots covered both her legs. She saw a doctor, and the next day while teaching class, her doctor called. Anna's blood test revealed her immune system was shutting down. Always positive, Anna asked what it was she had to do to make herself better.

Within hours Anna was being heavily sedated in preparation for a bone-marrow biopsy. The terrible news was delivered to Anna and husband Carlos. Anna was diagnosed with aplastic anemia. She would have to go in for chemotherapy and a bone-marrow transplant. The news hit Anna "like a ton of bricks. I was told the life I knew, I would never have again."

Fearing for her two sons, Anna's immediate concern was if aplastic anemia is hereditary. It is not. Aplastic anemia strikes two in every 2 million people. Anna's body had stopped producing red and white cells, which fight off diseases.

Her chance of survival was at 20 percent, which she says was "better than zero." She was admitted to Good Samaritan Hospital.

The probability of finding the right transplant match among her three sisters and one brother was 25 percent. Anna would have to wait an agonizing five days to see if any of her siblings were a match. On the night of the fifth day, Anna dreamed of her brother, Junior. "We were kids again. He was giving me a ride on his bike like he always had. He looked back at me and said, 'Don't worry, I'm going to take care of you'" The next day, the doctor confirmed what Anna had dreamed.

To prepare for the transplant, Anna would have to endure an excruciating stay in a germ-free room for approximately 45 days, where she would be subjected to heavy doses of chemotherapy to prepare her body to accept the transplant. "I couldn't imagine getting through 45 days of this," she said. So she took life by the hour, setting a clock next to her bed that would beep every hour. When times got worse, she would set her clock by the minute.

On September 11, 2001, Anna received the transplant. Her first recollection was that of her sister declaring, "We're being bombed." Anna watched as the second plane flew into the World Trade Center. She would remain glued to the television the remaining days in isolation. A year later, Anna's body began rejecting the transplant, so she would have to endure another stay in the germ-free room and get a stem-cell transplant. She has been in remission since 2002.

This experience has taught Anna to live life by the moment. She has also learned the importance of service, having been recently elected vice mayor for Tolleson. Though Anna's immune system continues to be a challenge, her positive take on this "fight for life" has made her immune to hopelessness.

From a funeral-home manager: Life is precious

While introducing himself to a large audience of teens, Eddie Lopez reaches into an empty casket and pulls out a bottle of water and takes a sip. "I'm always certain my water will be safe in there." A laugh emerges from the crowd.

He walks up to various teens and makes peculiar comments such as, "Do all the drugs you want; I need the money." "Drink and drive as often as you can; I need the money. Join a gang, in fact, join two; I need the money."

Unaccustomed to hearing reverse psychology, the audience eagerly tunes in to listen to the slender, thickly-mustached manager of Greenfield Funeral Home. Eddie then whips out what he fondly refers to as his "Blue Ribbon Award," a shiny plastic body bag. He points out how most teens who die of gunshot wounds are shot in the back while trying to flee. "This isn't Hollywood; there is nothing glamorous in getting shot. The purpose of this body bag is to secure all the different fluids that seep out of the body as a result of the wounds," he says.

He goes into some sobering statistics: Nearly 30,000 people die each year in Maricopa County. At his funeral home, 60 percent are between the ages of 14 and 29. "Most deaths occur after 10 p.m.

That's when you belong to me," he says. "And you know what the saddest part is? It's that most of them did it to themselves."

He shares poignant stories that drive home his point. One is of a boy angry at his parents' decision to move the family to another state. In a fit of rage, the boy stormed into his room and hanged himself. Evidence indicated the boy changed his mind, but it was too late. The boy died in a gruesome manner. "Always remember; suicide is a permanent solution to a temporary problem." Lopez tells the crowd.

His presentations educate the public about how different ethnic groups view death, cremation and burial ceremonies. He also delves into the business aspect of his field and how the deceased are prepared for burial. Lopez's biggest pet peeve is how our society avoids talking about death. He recalls how a beautifully dressed little girl came into his office one day holding tightly to a rose. She had not been told her mother had died, only that she was sleeping. Naturally, she thought her mom would awaken soon. "I had to explain to her that her mother had passed away and would not be returning." Later that day, Lopez noticed the rose lying next to the mother's urn. "I still have that rose today to remind me to make the most of life by not ignoring death."

"When we ignore death, we plunge into a false belief that life comes equipped with unlimited time, which results in us not making the most of our lives here on earth," Lopez says. This is the primary reason he volunteers his time on the speaking circuit. He concludes his presentation with a gift for everyone; a bracelet that reads, "Life is precious."

SEVEN

THE FACES OF IMMIGRATION

A death in a family, a change in perspective

Eddie Lopez still chokes up when he recounts the day 7-year-old Selena entered his life. A white confirmation dress and a tiara hung in the room. Eddie marveled at this little girl's beauty. She had long brown hair, long eyelashes and a perfect nose. Her fingernails were long and manicured. And her lips were moist. This usually is not the case after an autopsy. "She just looked like she was sleeping." Eddie says.

Selena had died in her mother's arms, from complications of asthma.

Though Selena was an American citizen, her parents, who had come to America illegally, resisted taking her to a doctor for fear of deportation. Instead, they had purchased her medicine at a local swap meet. "So much was on Selena's shoulders," Eddie recalls. "She was both translator and negotiator for the family."

Eddie, general manager for Crystal Rose Funeral Home in Tolleson, made several visits to Selena's home to make funeral arrangements. He met only with Selena's mother. Her father would not participate in the planning. What would anger Eddie most was seeing him hanging out with his buddies in the back alley, sporting a beer in his hand. "What an idiot!" Eddie thought. How could this guy be drinking, knowing his daughter had just died?

On the day of the service, Selena's father arrived early demanding to see his daughter. Eddie unhappily pointed the way. As the father approached the small white casket his legs gave way. He reached for Selena's hands. Tears gushed from his eyes, pouring onto Selena's tiny body. "What am I going to do now?" he cried. After some time, he asked the unthinkable. If he could hold Selena in his arms one last time! This was against policy, but those who mourn are not concerned with policy. Surprisingly, Eddie agreed. Soon Selena was in her father's arms.

As he sat in a chair, he rocked Selena back and forth singing her their song, *My Little Princess*. Eddie soon realized that he had violated the No. 1 rule of his profession. Don't pass judgment on how someone mourns the loss of a loved one. Perhaps we can learn from Eddie's experience about perceptions. Especially, as it relates to today's "illegal immigration" quandary. In the midst of the angry rhetoric, political posturing and dreadful government policies lies a little princess named Selena.

Happy Samuel's final word of the day: Adios!

Every day in my first-hour world history class, the day began with Samuel posting the school's word of the day on the board. All that was required was the posting of the word. But Samuel, a perpetual happy student, would go the extra mile. He would write the definition and declare the word a noun, verb, adjective or pronoun. It was nice to have someone take charge of a task that was clearly my responsibility as a high school teacher. But Samuel took on this challenge voluntarily without any prompting from anyone. So as human nature would have it, I came to expect this new service he was providing without any expectation of reward.

To see his rough exterior, one would think Samuel was older than he actually was. He was also more pleasant than he appeared. Forever pondering the world around him, at some point during class, Samuel invariably would make his way back to my desk from the front row where he sat, and would pose thought-provoking questions to me. During class discussions he would chime in with wisdom and humor that he had learned from his enrollment in life's school of hard knocks. He understood what it was like to be poor and grasped the promise of what a good education meant toward achieving the American Dream.

One day Samuel journeyed back to my desk. Only this time he did not pose a thought-provoking question. Instead, he informed me that he would be leaving soon. When asked where he would be going, Samuel responded, Puerto Peñasco, Mexico. I asked how long he planned on staying there. Samuel replied that he and his family would not be returning. He acknowledged being brought to America as a child. Samuel went on to say that his father, a landscaper, wanted to leave prior to the new employer sanctions law that took effect in January. Samuel's father was troubled by how difficult things had become for him, so the decision was made to return to Mexico.

Samuel and I didn't talk much about the situation after that. Things went on as usual for some time. Then came the day when I entered my classroom and noticed one empty desk in the front row and my white board void of the word of the day. This time it was my turn to contemplate all that's occurring with this illegal immigration quandary—from the employer sanctions law to the political circus occurring at Pruitt's Furniture in Phoenix. Many are caught in the crossfire.

For those who believe that illegal immigrants will self deport back home by removing the magnet that attracts them here, namely jobs, this is certainly one example of being right. But, no matter where one falls on the illegal immigration issue, one thing is certain: As the sun rises signaling a new day in Arizona, it finds itself less one landscaper and one young dreamer. And I find myself pondering the word of the day.

Couple caught in the immigration maze

Newlyweds Justin and Esther Allen arrived at the border checkpoint in Nogales on schedule. Justin's father was at the wheel. The traffic was busy and chaotic. Border Patrol agents approached. When asked if everyone in the vehicle was an American, Justin, a U.S. citizen, responded, "No." He gestured to Esther and told them she was a Mexican citizen but that she had a visa. Without explanation, Esther was forbidden to cross. Shocked, Justin told them Esther was his wife.

This made matters worse. Tensions mounted as they were soon surrounded by a slew of agents. After removing Esther's luggage, Justin's father drove through the checkpoint and left the newlyweds behind. As they fought through the traffic, people began honking their horns and mocking them. "It was the most humiliating thing I've ever experienced." Justin recalls.

The next morning, Esther, terrified and humiliated, returned home to Guadalajara. Justin headed back to the border checkpoint. Reminiscent from a scene in *Born in East LA*, an agent recognized Justin and would not let him cross. He tried again later without success. Then a Mexican man covered in tattoos approached Justin with an offer to get him across for $500 pesos. Desperate, Justin agreed. They stood in line, allowing others to cut ahead, and when the opportunity came, the man summoned Justin to a particular agent and he was allowed through.

Eighteen months later, Justin's journey through the immigration maze has resulted in great frustration for the Goodyear resident. "The Immigration Service Staff consistently gives me the wrong information," he says. "One day I was provided with a packet of forms to fill out, which turned out to be for Cuban refugees seeking asylum in America. It's one wrong hoop after another . . . Prior to getting married we visited the American consulate in Mexico and they told us it would be no problem getting Esther across." In fact, eight months ago, the Immigration Service could not find their paper work.

Of the estimated 12 million people currently living in the United States illegally, 40 percent simply allowed their visas to expire. Esther believes that our immigration policy forces people into citizenship. Like many, Esther has no desire to become a U.S. citizen. She simply wants to be able to travel legally between the two countries.

Being apart for various lengths of time has put a strain on the young newlyweds. Both possess college degrees in International Business.

Esther's experience has left her traumatized, as she is currently being treated for depression. But they remain determined to do things the right way. If only someone could point them in that direction.

EIGHT

POLITICAL PHILOSOPHY/STRATEGY

We have plenty in common, so let's talk

My columns have appeared in *The Arizona Republic* for six years, and I consider it an honor to have this great opportunity to share my thoughts on topics ranging from the political to the personal.

Although perhaps at times you may not have agreed with what I've said, it is refreshing when you respond to my columns respectfully and with statesmanship.

Unfortunately, respect and statesmanship are sorely lacking in today's political arena. Opposing sides are locked in perpetual win-at-any-costs duels without any prospect of wisdom seeing the light of day.

Your responses to my columns have taught me that we can accomplish much if we just tone down the vitriolic rhetoric.

I take your comments to heart whether they agree with me or not. Yes, there have been the occasional comments that failed the respect criteria, but they have come in such rare numbers as should be hardly mentioned.

And, no, this is not goodbye. You'll continue to see my columns, but I've been given a new challenge that offers me the opportunity to express my thoughts through the airwaves.

My talk-radio show, "From the Roots Up With Randy Camacho," will focus on thought-provoking content that proves no matter what political, racial, or religious persuasion we may belong to, we have more in common than we think. I will be incorporating many of The Arizona Republic columns I've written over the years, including in-depth stories, and relating them to today's pressing issues, both locally and nationally.

The radio show will air Saturdays from 11 a.m. to noon on KXXT-AM (1010). The show begins June 5 and runs through Oct. 30. It will also run live via the Internet and will be available through KXXT's website for audio listening and webcam replay throughout the week.

I don't claim to have all the answers, but I do have a strong desire to help create a community of listeners that will find solace, inspiration, hope and a new-found perspective of life and the world we live in.

Last year, I received an award from the Arizona Press Club. David Carpenter of the Associated Press in Chicago had this to say about my columns: "An excellent storyteller who makes you want to read to the very end to find out how the columns come out."

I hope you tune in to the very end to find out how the radio show comes out.

Getting past gatekeepers isn't easy

One of the most thought-provoking pieces of advice I've received came from Raul Aguirre, an advertising company owner in southeastern Arizona. When we met, he said to me: "If you want to get anywhere in life, you've got to learn how to get past the gatekeepers." Gatekeepers come in many forms. It can be the automated phone system that prohibits you from speaking to a live person or the administrative assistant that keeps you from the person in charge. It can be the public relations coordinator that denies you access to that high-profile person or simply anyone that's in a strategic position to block one's ability to progress.

For Raul, gatekeepers have come in the form of outreach employees. Raul doesn't much care for the word "outreach" as well. He views it as "demeaning." He said, "If I want to talk to the head of Arizona Public Service, for example, I want to talk to the head, not an outreach person. That person's just in the way."

In Raul's line of business, access is paramount and he fully understands that the shortest distance from Point A to Point B is a straight line. During his tenure as a minority business owner, Raul has experienced many detours along the path to the office of the decision maker. At times Raul managed to break through only to be redirected to the outreach person.

My experience with a gatekeeper occurred when I was trying to meet with some leaders of a first-responder organization during my run for Congress. A person whom I had grown up with was the community outreach person for this organization. About every other word he spoke was "bro" or "yeah, bro." As I talked with him to arrange a meeting with his superiors, my campaign director also was doing the same thing. As it turned out, my campaign director was able to arrange the meeting while the outreach person continued to assure me that he was on it. I never heard from him.

There are many who may assert that we ourselves play the role of gatekeeper by allowing our doubts to keep us from achieving success. I would not take it that far, but I will say that many of us do deal with various gatekeepers from time to time. Simply put, when you have to walk a crooked line in order to move forward most likely you've had to maneuver past a gatekeeper.

Complacency toward the gatekeeper has become a relatively new "freedom" society seems to be accepting and this trend will continue until society declares its freedom by making it more difficult for gatekeepers to easily possess the key.

Raul's advice continues to ring with me. One day I came across a representative from the governor's office during a formal dinner. She asked, "Is there anything you'd like for me to say to the governor for you?" I thought for a moment then kindly replied, "Just tell her hi for me."

Civil disobedience is a peaceful way to fight injustice

My father's lifelong inability to grasp the biblical enigma—should one strike you on the right cheek, offer them the left—was marked by as much frustration as many of us are currently feeling about our never-ending immigration quandary.

With the nation's attention centered squarely on Arizona and Senate Bill 1070, protesters unleashed a barrage of various acts of defiance this summer ranging from chaining themselves to doors, to blocking traffic and purposely provoking police into arresting them. And they are preparing for an encore of various forms of civil disobedience.

But is civil disobedience just about protesters getting arrested or is there more to it? Mohandas K. Gandhi, the father of civil disobedience, fought a lifelong battle to free India from British rule. After many years of struggle, independence finally arrived in 1947. Gandhi employed a non-violent movement of non-cooperation including boycotts, denouncing British customs, fostering a return to Indian culture, and leading a 200-mile march to the Indian Sea to make salt, publicly defying British law that forbade it. Gandhi's peaceful fight for justice later served as an inspiration for future leaders like the Rev. Martin Luther King Jr., Cesar Chavez and Nelson Mandela.

The essence of civil disobedience parallels with the biblical passage of turning the other cheek. Gandhi believed that something happens in human nature that makes it difficult to continue striking someone physically if they are not striking back. This results in the aggressor's respect increasing for the person demonstrating they will not engage in violence nor will they retreat or be turned away. Civil disobedience in its purest form is another method of fighting. Much the same as a soldier going off to war; there is nothing passive about it. The civil resisters demonstrate the injustice through their pain and suffering just as pain and suffering exists in all battles. An example of this principle was exhibited in the 1960s, when Americans watched with dismay as bloodied civil-rights activists, defying Jim Crow laws in the South, were dragged out of private eating establishments that would not serve "colored" people.

Just as in war, the civil resister sacrifices much in the fight for justice. Mandela languished in prison for 27 years before he rose to become leader of South Africa. Gandhi and King fell to assassins' bullets. Chavez died as a result of the various fasts he endured in his fight for farmworkers' rights.

Leaders and groups fighting for immigration rights have not grasped the essence of civil disobedience nor do they understand what they are fighting for. Perhaps it's because the movement is lacking a charismatic leader that can bring the diverse factions together. For a true battle of wills to commence, there has to emerge a leader that can articulate a vision, is willing to accept the risks, and lives in accordance to the message.

Dems need to shift strategy

The sea of losses in the 2010 midterm elections left Democrats across the country licking their wounds and wondering what to make of the thrashing. Certainly, Democratic casualties will mount for party leaders nationwide when they face the wrath of grass-roots party members in upcoming reorganization meetings. Undoubtedly, heads are going to roll. That cannot be avoided, nor should it be. It's survival of the fittest in this political environment, and Democrats must evolve or risk becoming an endangered species.

Pundits surmise that Democrats' lack of a national message coupled with a slumping economy was to blame for the legislative and congressional defeats. I do not believe it is that simple. The problem for the Democratic Party is not just the lack of a cohesive message but its organizational structure. It has been operating much like a social network such as Facebook or Twitter, in which lines of communication run sideways. Such a structure works well for spreading information but not for developing it. For the Democratic Party to reverse the trend for future elections, it must begin operating more like a hierarchal organization with a central authority, similar to the 1960s civil-rights movement.

New Yorker columnist Malcolm Gladwell recently wrote that social networks are not beneficial to producing the kind of courageous activism that brought about the sit-ins at segregated diners because social networks require very little in way of true sacrifice. They, instead, ask members to complete tasks that require little effort, such as signing online petitions. Gladwell also points out that networks struggle to reach consensus or set goals, "They can't think strategically; they are chronically prone to conflict and error. How do you make difficult choices about tactics or strategy or philosophical direction when everyone has an equal say . . . . Networks don't have a centralized leadership structure and clear lines of authority."

An organizational hierarchy is precisely what the civil-rights movement possessed, from the Rev. Martin Luther King Jr. to the NAACP to its local churches. The Democratic Party's design is hierarchal, but only in theory not in practice. Like social networks, today's Democratic Party is leaderless and without direction. Tasks and responsibilities sprawl infinitely in lateral directions with no central authority to design philosophy and to articulate a narrative that connects to everyday Americans.

An efficient central authority generates, what I term high-stakes activism, the sense that success in the next election is a matter of life and death, as was the case for Democrats in the 2006 elections when opposition to the Iraq War was at its peak. High-stakes activism, with its high level of concern, produces passion and a strong morale essential for election victories. That's how the midterm elections were perceived by the "tea partyers." As they saw it, they were willing to sacrifice to take back their country. And for civil-rights activists, they viewed their cause as noble and worth dying for.

Democrats need to act with the same moral urgency of the civil-rights and the tea-party movements. This type of high-stakes activism is what the Democratic Party needs to win in the future, thus guaranteeing it does not become an endangered species.

'None of the above' should be an option on ballot

Have you ever found yourself on Election Day trying to decide between two candidates you were not crazy about? Maybe it was because both were more concerned with slinging mud at each other than thoughtfully discussing the issues you care about. Or perhaps you were familiar with one candidate, someone you disliked passionately, but had never heard of the other. That's because the political party the other candidate belonged to deemed the race unwinnable and put up anyone with a pulse to run.

Such is the case today. Voters either have to pick between the lesser of two evils or an unknown commodity. It's like having to pick something to wear from a dirty basket of laundry. But, what if you had a third choice? Not a person but a choice. How about "none of the above"?

How much clout would your vote have if you had the ability to say to both political parties, "Give me someone better!" when there are few good choices on the ballot? And what if "none of the above" were to win? It would require a special election that would force both parties to appeal to a broader electorate rather than the few lying on the extreme fringes of both political spectrums.

Further, "none of the above" would not run those annoying campaign ads or say anything to get elected. It would be on the ballot simply as a fallback for voters when they want to exercise their right to use it. If we are going to have tax-subsidized state elections, why not present voters with "none of the above" as a choice in primary and general elections? It would certainly make every election more competitive. "None of the above" would also ensure no more politicians run unopposed.

In fact, why limit ourselves? We should do the same in Washington. Consider the U.S. Senate race of 2010 in Connecticut where voters were presented with two stark but unattractive choices, state Attorney General Richard Blumenthal and businesswoman Linda McMahon. Blumenthal spoke often of his service in the Vietnam War and even insinuated he had experienced the "indignities" Vietnam vets suffered at the hands of antiwar protesters. It was all good except for one thing: Blumenthal never served in Vietnam. In fact, he put in for several deferments from 1965 to 1970 to avoid going to war. Linda McMahon made her fortune as a professional-wrestling promoter. Of course, the campaign season resembled a political version of "Wrestlemania" where voters felt as helpless as a pro-wrestling referee.

How would the race have turned out had "none of the above" been on the ballot?

This "none of the above" idea is not meant to get rid of the two-party system, but to enhance it by making it more vibrant. It would compel both parties to appeal to the broader electorate. That means the issues important to you would surface and become part of the political discourse. Perhaps then, we can find the elusive statesman we've been looking for.

We seem to be yearning for something new and meaningful. When our Founding Fathers embarked on establishing our country, they were venturing into the unknown. Like our Founding Fathers, we must do the same without changing the foundation of our country, which is rooted in freedom of choice. Instead of continuing to be locked in political purgatory, it's time to shake things up. The message should be clear to both parties, "Put up your best, or else!"

Next U.S. senator needs passion, positive outlook

In April, 2012, I will serve on a search committee to select the next president of a community college. The selection process begins by developing a position profile that specifies the traits the search team will be looking for that match the mission goals of the college. The timeline requires that this part of the process be completed prior to selecting potential candidates.

Imagine if the selection process for the U.S. Senate seat being vacated by Jon Kyl operated much like the hiring of a college president. What traits would the search committee—voters—be looking for in the next U.S. senator from Arizona? Before the ink had dried on Kyl's retirement announcement, potential candidates began churning out of the political vortex from both Republican and Democratic circles, before a position profile had been established.

Probably the most important factor for voters to contemplate is what it takes to be a great leader. Allan Gregg, a well-respected pollster, once told TV talk-show host Chris Matthews that every great leader possesses three key elements.

*Motive. You know why they have entered public service.

For John F. Kennedy, it was his call for volunteerism and for America to reach the moon by the end of the 1960s. For Ronald Reagan, it was his can-do spirit and the belief that the Cold War could be won. For Franklin Delano Roosevelt, it was his belief that government plays a role in bringing about economic stability.

*Passion. It is the strong feelings that demonstrate firmness in one's heart for the values that make the person. It's the emotional will that captures the heart of the public. It's that sense of joy in serving while not taking life for granted.

*Spontaneity. According to Matthews, it's when a leader shows what they've got during that unscripted moment away from consultants and handlers.

It is when that certain genuineness is revealed, demonstrating their sense of "realness." For Bill Clinton, it was the comfort and inspiration he provided for the families of the victims of the Oklahoma bombing. For George W. Bush, it was his "I hear you" response while standing on the rubble of the Twin Towers. You may say that's a lot to ask from our next senator. But consider that this opportunity does not come around too often, and we've had two senators from Arizona come within arm's reach of the presidency.

The last piece of the position profile is the candidate's disposition toward the future. Is the person positive about it? For example, when they look at the border, do they simply see a fence and a way to secure votes? Or do they see two distinct economies that must find commonality that ensures America's security and fosters the type of prosperity where potential border-crossers elect to stay home with their families? Do they see a new brand of American education and ingenuity, an America thriving in the new high-tech economy that exports American products not American jobs? Lastly, do they see America's promise as it relates to us and throughout the world? Now that the position profile for the Senate seat has been established, let the search begin.

'The Process' can be deadly

Imagine applying for a job where you were led to believe your chances for obtaining it were excellent. Your hopes were raised even further when you were informed that you were one of the finalists. You interviewed one final time.

When the decision came down, the one offered the job was . . . . Somebody else! As time went on, you came to discover that the procedure had been staged and that it already had been decided long before the interviews who—qualified or unqualified—was going to get the job. Unfortunately, you've just become victim of "The Process."

"The Process" takes on many forms with only one intention, to accomplish its goal. It is the ultimate example of the ends justifying the means. In your case, no law was broken and any wrongdoing would be difficult to prove. "The Process" is used to conceal the true reality under the guise of openness and diversity. It can be used to either discriminate or reverse discriminate in the job market. It may also be used to keep small businesses from gaining access to major contracts.

Yet those who engage in the practice swear that it's fair. They've always counted on one thing. That folks affected by "The Process" are so busy with their lives that they'll either forget or simply shake their heads and move on.

Recently, voters in the City of Goodyear rejected Prop 400, which would have made fire sprinklers mandatory in new homes. This was certainly an unexpected result for those backing the proposition. Goodyear Mayor Jim Cavanaugh initially hoped through "The Process" to take this issue back to the voters again sometime in the future. He since has abandoned that idea—Wisely—in favor of a citizens committee to study fire-safety alternatives and strategies.

On the national political scene, it was discovered recently that five of the eight top Federal Emergency Management Agency officials came to their positions with hardly any experience in dealing with natural disasters. When Hurricane Katrina struck New Orleans, the unexpected breach of the levies exposed how through "The Process," incompetent people came to hold such important posts over those that were more qualified. Unfortunately, this cronyism resulted in loss of lives, property and tremendous human suffering. Whether in the job market, the business world, or political arena, the "The Process" beat goes on, and so does its civilized brutality.

NINE

POLITICS IN ARIZONA

It shouldn't be a crime to be a Good Samaritan

One photo stopped me dead in my tracks as I was going through the Newseum a few years ago. The Washington, D.C., museum is known for its display of Pulitzer Prize-winning photography. In this stunning photo, an emaciated half-naked African baby huddled facedown in the desert wilderness with no human in sight. Several feet away stood a vulture on the ground patiently waiting for the baby to die. The picture, taken by South African photo journalist Kevin Carter, causes many to pause somberly. In 1993, Carter received permission from the Sudan government to cover the extreme famine there. But he had to agree to the government's demand that he not interfere with the events he would chronicle.

So when Carter happened upon this baby, he snapped the photo and left. He won the coveted Pulitzer Prize for it but was heavily criticized when it was discovered that he had not helped the baby in any way. If he had, however, Carter would have risked being apprehended by government officials and having the photo confiscated. That would have kept the world from witnessing the famine in its truest form, ending any possibility of worldwide outcry from the photo. A few months after winning the Pulitzer, Carter fell into a deep depression and committed suicide.

During the past 15 years, a similar human tragedy has been unfolding in America's Southwestern desert, much like Sudan. More than 5,000 men, women and children have died crossing the desert border into the United States. In Arizona, 206 migrants died in 2009. But in this case, there are no compelling photos to create a public outcry. Pictures of desert deaths continue to be kept from the public to spare them the trauma of seeing such graphic images of the many who have succumbed to the elements. Being deprived of this experience has warped the perception of the public and lawmakers, resulting in a failure to view this humanitarian problem in its truest form.

Senate Bill 1070, introduced by Sen. Russell Pearce, is an example of this warped perception. A provision in the bill makes it a crime for a U.S. citizen to render any type of aid to an illegal immigrant; that could be construed as harboring or transporting. Under this bill, should one happen upon a migrant child stranded in the desert, it would be unlawful to transport the child. Rendering any aid could be viewed as harboring.

If this bill goes forward and Gov. Jan Brewer signs it into law, Arizona would forbid an act of compassion by a Good Samaritan and would be acting no differently than Sudan did when it forbade Carter from helping a dying baby. Perhaps the time has come to encourage the best photojournalists to chronicle the humanitarian tragedy that continues to play out in our desert. Maybe then a picture will emerge that transcends hatred and creates the public outcry that shames lawmakers on both sides of the border into creating policy that finally brings an end to this human calamity.

Feel-good legislation doesn't help—it hurts

A former college instructor of mine, who is a principal in the Scottsdale Elementary school district, once proclaimed, "Never make a rule that you're not willing to enforce!" Failure to do so leads to a breakdown in student discipline and campus morale. Several years ago in a Valley high school, a victory horn sounded the day chewing gum was officially banned from school. At first, students complied, until they witnessed the school's inability and unwillingness to enforce the new rule. Eventually, chewing gum filled the mouths of the majority of the student population.

Most teachers lost faith in the administration's ability to enforce the rule. Yet, a few idealistic teachers made a futile attempt to enforce the rule and invented their own punishment for the gum-chewers. In the end, the no-gum-chewing rule proved to be nothing more than a feel-good-rule, long in symbolism but short in substance.

Lawmakers are not immune from the feel-good bug. They revel when feel-good laws are passed, giving the appearance that important work is being accomplished to appease a frustrated public. Feel-good laws absorb energy that could otherwise be used to solve many of today's pressing problems such as our state budget, the economy and illegal immigration.

When speed cameras began flashing photos of speeding motorists, many Arizonans long frustrated with speeders welcomed the new technology with great enthusiasm. However, an ominous cloud has formed enveloping our judicial system in the process. According to a recent study, approximately, three of every four motorists ticketed by photo enforcement have not paid their fines. This means that the state now has the monumental task of process serving thousands of ticketed motorists with official notices to appear in court before the 120-day deadline. As a result, the court caseload has skyrocketed by more than 60 percent, leaving many to question how effective photo enforcement will be in the future and whether our state has the ability and willingness to uphold photo enforcement and the consequences that accompany it.

The federal government's failure to control the illegal-immigration flow has created a great deal of public anger that has prompted rogue politicians such as Sheriff Joe Arpaio and states like Arizona to invent their own brand of enforcement. In an effort to curb illegal immigration, Arizona passed the employer-sanctions law that went into effect on Jan.1, 2008. It was said to be one of the toughest immigration laws in the country. State lawmaker Russell Pearce, who helped champion the law, made appearances on various news media outlets to celebrate its passage. The law would suspend or revoke the license of any business that "knowingly" hires illegal immigrants. But the word "knowingly" has shown to be very difficult to prove.

After nearly two years since the law went into effect, County Attorney Andrew Thomas recently announced the indictment of a local business believed to be in violation of the employer-sanctions law. Ironically, Raphael Libardi of Brazil, a business owner of a granite company, may be an illegal immigrant himself. He is also facing other charges including identity theft. Since the enactment of the employer-sanctions law, 21 investigations have taken place in Maricopa County; so far, not one business has been fined or had its license revoked.

It is clear that many Americans are distressed about the current direction of our country. Unfortunately, when feel-good-laws are permitted to see the light of day because of the public's haste to solve problems, they allow lawmakers to turn the focus from their responsibility to provide clear, pragmatic solutions to the real challenges facing America today. By repeatedly giving into this distraction, Americans have created this dragon; and only they can slay the monstrosity.

Mixed messages a smoke screen for hypocrisy

A political cartoon in a local newspaper featured a fence along the U.S.-Mexican border. On the American side, facing Mexico, were two signs in proximity to each other nailed to fence posts. One sign read "No Trespassing" while the other read "Now Hiring." Humor can travel vast distances when it speaks the truth. But it does prompt this question: Has America become a nation of mixed messages?

According to a recent study, 150 members of Congress "currently receive government-funded; government-administered single-payer health care." Among these members, 54 are Republicans adamantly opposed to this same type of health care for the rest of America. Among the fifty-four notables are Arizona Senators Jon Kyl and John McCain.

The Wall Street Journal recently reported that the Obama administration has agreed in principle to providing $2 billion in aid to Brazil's state-owned oil company Petrobras in order to "finance exploration of the huge offshore discovery in Brazil's Tupi oil field in the Santos Basin near Rio de Janeiro." Interestingly, during his presidential campaign, Obama declared his opposition to offshore drilling, calling it a "scheme."

Maricopa County Attorney Andrew Thomas and Sheriff Joe Arpaio held a joint press conference on Nov. 18 to announce the first complaint filed against a business believed to be in violation of the state employer-sanctions law, which became effective in January 2008. The law would suspend or revoke the license of any business that "knowingly" hires illegal immigrants. An undercover informant hired by the Sheriff's Office wore a hidden camera and recorded Michelle Hardas, manager of an art factory in Scottsdale, attempting to hire illegal workers. Ironically, the undercover informant hired by the Sheriff's Office is an illegal immigrant.

This fall, the Avondale City Council voted to name a water-treatment facility in honor of former council member Chuck Wolf. Wolf graciously accepted the honor. Yet, last year, before Wolf resigned from the council, he had this to say regarding a measure to name a city library honoring long-time resident Sam Garcia: "Naming structures or parks after individuals opens up Pandora's Box. If we allow this to happen, then anybody will have something named after them."

State Rep. Steve Montenegro, R-Litchfield Park, was among various legislators who shadowed school administrators in order to see firsthand the day-to-day operation of our state's schools. After completing his visit in Avondale school district, Montenegro stated, "Now I have a good grip, a good understanding, of the tools the district needs for each school." Thanksgiving week, Montenegro voted to cut an additional $144 million from the state's education budget, including a measure ending teacher seniority.

Mixed messages abound. Kenney Chesney sings "Everybody wants to go to heaven, but nobody wants to go now" in a song that pokes fun at Americans' propensity for mixed messages. But, there is little to chuckle about when mixed messages reveal a glaring hypocrisy. Perhaps 17th century philosopher John Locke summed it up best when he said the actions of people are the best interpreters of their thoughts.

Immigration reform: Arizona can lead the way

Soft taco shell or hard taco shell? A recent TV commercial has customers debating which way to go. Then, in Spanish, a little girl replies, "¿Por qué no los dos?" Why not both? Proponents of SB 1070 assert that over 70 percent of Arizonans are in favor of it. Surprisingly, a poll conducted by Lake Research Partners and Public Opinions Policy also indicates a strong favorability among SB 1070 supporters for comprehensive immigration reform. According to the survey, 84 percent of Arizonans support reform that includes a pathway to citizenship for undocumented immigrants while 78 percent nationally favor reform. Comprehensive immigration reform was defined in the poll as "Beefing up border security and creating a tough pathway to citizenship that involves undergoing a background check, paying taxes, learning English and waiting in line."

So why can't we have both border security and a beginning pathway to legalization in Arizona? There is little to keep us from implementing our own version of comprehensive immigration reform, which could be a way for qualified undocumented immigrants to become Arizona residents. Respondents, by a large number, said responsibility of immigration rests with the federal government but favor "state action" over the inaction of the feds. The qualifications for state residency could include a certain number of years in Arizona, a clean criminal record, competency in English, and a history of being gainfully employed and contributing to society.

Why limit ourselves to an enforcement-only mentality? Besides, an enforcement-only strategy has resulted in toothless measures such as the employer-sanctions law. In this regard, our state mirrors the inaction of our federal government because it fails to add a component to take away the incentive for breaking the law, namely legally matching willing employees with willing employers. As for securing our border, if it's as bad as they say, there's little preventing Gov. Jan Brewer from deploying our National Guard in Arizona to the border.

Immigration reform legislators and activists should turn their focus away from Washington, because Congress currently does not have the stomach for it. Instead, their passion should rest on making reform happen in our state.

Our desire to see the world in simple black and white terms has resulted in a failure to determine the negative impact of enforcement-only legislation, such as Arizona's national image problem and the attraction of well-funded hate groups that help craft our legislation.

It's time to create legislation that does not mirror existing federal law but can work as a shining example of how to effectively deal with the illegal-immigration issue firmly but compassionately. And if Congress ever develops the will to pass reform, Arizona would be well ahead of the nation. So, Arizona: Why not both?

A peaceful backlash against hate

As we watched the vast white-clothed tide of humanity gather and move at a glacier's pace along Grand Avenue to the state Capitol on Monday, it signaled that the battle to capture America's heart has officially begun. In their zeal to find an election-year wedge issue, Republican lawmakers found it fashionable to declare open season on "illegal aliens" with angry rhetoric bordering on pocket bigotry and by playing a political game of one-upmanship for the title of "Toughest on Illegals."

Leading the fray and speaking like someone running for Congress for the first time, Rep. J.D. Hayworth, R-Ariz., has attempted to make his mark by writing a book titled *Whatever It Takes* in which he advocates immediate deportation of all of the estimated 12 million individuals living in America illegally. After all, it was safe to go after people who could not defend themselves politically. However, the tipping point against this political posturing occurred when a proposal in Congress aimed to make it a felony to reside in America illegally or to render aid to an "illegal" crossing the desert.

When cornered, a prey's only option is to fight back. In this case the fight was taken to the streets in a peaceful, diplomatic fashion to highlight a flawed immigration policy and a disjointed logic in Congress. There is little doubt that this backlash may prove detrimental to the Republican Party in the future. Although too early to determine what impact the immigration issue will have on the 2006 national and state elections, political experts believe that if any is to occur it will not happen until the 2008 presidential election, when many of the young marchers will become active voters. Republicans may experience a short-term spike in public support, which means they will likely retain control of the House and the Senate both nationally and statewide. However, for Republicans, this may prove to be an ominous sign of things to come.

So they marched—young families, small children, frail elderly and rambunctious teens. In an era where Republicans tout family values and morality, Monday's peaceful march was truly an inspiring display of family, faith and patriotism. Ironically, these values may cost Republicans in the future. Consider the numerous stories: From a woman who came to America illegally 30 years ago eventually earning citizenship who proudly displayed a poster board with pictures of her two sons currently serving our country in Iraq, to the restaurant worker who lost a day's pay in order to attend the march, to the families who tearfully marched in honor of the loved ones they had lost to the Arizona desert.

The constant barrage of offensive legislative proposals during this open season by Republicans has acted to dehumanize illegal immigrants. But look into the crowd and you'll see that these so called "illegal aliens" who took part in this historic march are human beings who have individual faces of hard-working, loyal and honest people who are clearly part of America's future.

Franks isn't doing his job

Tired of the endless back-ups on Interstate 10 in the Southwest Valley? In order to accelerate the expansion of I-10 from Dysart Road to Cotton Lane, the Goodyear City Council has hired Triadvocates, at taxpayers' expense, to lobby U.S. Sen. Jon Kyl and U.S. Rep. Trent Franks to gain funding support for this effort. It can certainly be appreciated that the City Council is doing whatever it takes to move the I-10 expansion ahead of schedule. But why on earth would they spend taxpayer money to lobby Franks when this is the very district he represents and he should be as concerned about the traffic problems on I-10 as the residents of the Southwest Valley? Shouldn't securing federal highway funds already be on the agenda of an elected official such as Franks?

Does a communication and collaboration void exist between Franks and the local governments of the Southwest Valley? Surely Franks is aware that securing federal transportation funds for the I-10 expansion is a must. After all, this is a safety, economic and quality of life issue. Adding more lanes would help attract major businesses to the Southwest Valley, cut down on the length of a morning or evening commute and allow interstate commerce to flow more freely. No doubt Franks concurs. Or does he?

In 2005, U.S. Rep. John Shadegg refused federal funds granted for the I-17 and Happy Valley Road reconstruction project because he opposes "earmarks" attached to spending bills. He considers earmarks "pork." In fact, Franks voted against a federal transportation bill that provided the necessary funds for the Hoover Dam Bypass. Perhaps he does not recognize the economic and security issues that his district faces. This might explain why Goodyear felt the need to hire a firm to lobby Franks. Goodyear would be better served by challenging Franks to adequately represent the residents of his district, not lobby him at taxpayer expense. So the next time you find yourself parked on the Southwest Valley I-10, ask yourself this question: Is it "pork" or is it "baloney?"

A magical vision solves our transit problem

I found myself nodding off late one afternoon at Leaps Coffee House, thinking of our transportation woes in the Southwest Valley. There was a magic wand in my hand, or so I thought. And standing before me was former Litchfield Park Mayor Woody Thomas, dressed in a wizard outfit, or so I imagined. With some degree of skepticism, I handed Thomas the magic wand and asked him to come up with a series of solutions to solve our transportation problems.

Elated, the man with a magical resume said he was excited for the opportunity. He has served on the Transportation Policy Committee, an influential group of mayors and private citizens within the Maricopa Association of Governments, and served a stint as the vice-chairman of MAG, a regional planning body consisting of the Valley's mayors. He also has chaired the Arizona Appraisers Coalition, is a certified general real estate appraiser and is past president of TQM (Total Quality Management), a state employee association formed in 1974 to improve the way our government functions. "As we grow, the opportunity for a solid transportation plan diminishes," he reminded me.

In other words you only get one shot at getting it right (even with a magic wand). He mentioned that developers are earning a sizable profit of up to 40 percent on the sale of single family homes, and that affordable housing has been traded for a sound transportation plan. With his magic wand, he created Solution No. 1—"an environment for responsible growth" in which developers refuse to build in areas without a transportation plan.

Next was Solution No. 2 to resolve the dangerous mix of trucks and cars on Interstate-10 and State Route 85 in the Southwest Valley. He separated all the truck and auto traffic. The I-10 reliever, a proposed parallel freeway to I-10 but farther south, allowed truck traffic to flow in and out of the industrial corridor ending at Loop 202 and 55th Avenue. The original I-10 was for autos only. Talk about relief!

Solution No. 3: By using existing rail lines, Woody created a commuter train that ran from Palo Verde and ended at 4th Avenue and Jackson in downtown Phoenix, with stops in Buckeye, the Phoenix-Goodyear Airport, Tolleson and 35th Avenue. Further, he buried the double track rail lines 20-30 feet at the Phoenix Goodyear connection to keep it from interfering with commercial train traffic. Total travel time from Goodyear to 4th Avenue and Jackson: 30 minutes. According to Thomas, adding a double track of rail line is equivalent to adding 21 lanes of highway.

Solution No. 4: He added another commuter train with five stops from 167th and Grand avenues to downtown Phoenix. He reminded me: "When it comes to Cave Creek, Carefree, Scottsdale and Paradise Valley; their centers of employment are all within one mile of a rail connection; the same train system can be added there if you wish."

My imagination came back to Earth, and I realized Woody Thomas was sitting across from me in plain clothes, gesturing with my biscotti in his right hand. There was no magic wand; only practical solutions to an age-old problem that does not require magic—just a magical vision and the courage to say, "Why not?"

TEN

ARIZONA'S EDUCATION CONFLICT

Schools are on right path

As a high school history teacher, I feel a certain apprehension at the start of every school year. I hope that the content and skills I'm teaching my students are appropriate in preparing them for the future. Earlier this summer, I had the pleasure of participating in a program that allows educators of various grade levels to collaborate with the business sector in communicating the personal and educational skills the "real world" is looking for in prospective employees.

Partners Advancing Student Success is a program designed by Motorola in partnership with Arizona Public Service Co. Nearly 30 businesses and organizations from the West Valley took part in PASS 2006. Our week began with an orientation, which concluded with us being divided into several groups. We were then assigned a list of businesses to visit. My group visited a bottling company in Tolleson, a public works department, a bank in Buckeye and an automotive repair business in Litchfield Park.

Other groups visited non-profit organizations, resorts and high-tech businesses. Every business that we toured was prepared for our arrival. Many expressed their appreciation for what we do as educators. They were very upfront about the characteristics they desire in prospective employees. So, parents and guardians, heed their advice.

First, the business world wants our children to be team players. They stressed that in real life one may not particularly like a fellow colleague but that does not mean they could not still function as a team. To accentuate this concept of teamwork, our groups were given unassembled bicycles and asked to assemble them without speaking a word. All groups gestured their way toward successfully assembling these bikes. There was a great sense of pride among us when we completed our task and were further elated to learn that these bikes were going to be donated to a non-profit organization of our choice.

Second, that our children be problem solvers. Countless times we heard of cases where technology was not readily available in the work field requiring employees to calculate numbers or to solve problems without the use of a calculator, computer or device. Third, and most importantly, the business world wants our children to be people of good character. It was stressed that moral and ethical strength was a major component to a successful employee. Upon completion of the program, we concluded that many of the educational and personal skills corporate America is requiring of its prospective employees are already being taught in our schools. Unfortunately, it seems the critics of public education have yet to receive the memo.

It's war: Education in Arizona under attack

"I never thought I'd see the day when things would get this bad," our high-school principal said at a staff meeting after our district failed to obtain voter approval last month for a budget override. "And I hate to say it, but things are going to get worse." The somber address came a day after the school board voted to terminate 92 positions in the Tolleson Union High School

District. Our superintendent said this is only the first wave of the tsunami; there are more cuts to come. To make matters worse, the state Legislature recently voted to cut an additional $776 million from the education budget.

The override's failure was not due to a lack of effort. Volunteers canvassed neighborhoods knocking on doors and handing out literature. The Continue the Progress campaign also raised money and generated numerous phone calls. The override failed by 304 votes out of 6,824 cast. With three devastating budget cuts at the state level, many school districts are sinking in financial quicksand. And schools that fail to obtain voter approval of budget overrides, such as my district, have sunk even farther.

Make no mistake: Education is in a state of war; it's fighting for its right to exist, and most importantly, with the nature of the intense political climate with which it has to operate daily, education is fighting a war with itself. For education to have a shot at surviving, it must achieve three major victories over the next six months.

First is the passage of Proposition 100, the one-cent sales tax, which will be going to voters May 18. Two-thirds of the funding derived from the tax is set to be allocated toward education. Many schools will still be in the hole should the measure pass, but it will help fill the gap.

Second, is the passage of budget-override measures going to voters in November. Peoria school district will be one of those districts. Education's war against itself is epitomized in Peoria where a school-board member who is running for a seat in the Arizona House is actively attempting to defeat Prop. 100.

Third, is the public electing sensible lawmakers that support our educational institutions and will work to make them more efficient by developing pragmatic solutions, free of political demagoguery, to make education better.

Not long ago, I was golfing with a friend of mine. When it was my turn to hit, I could not see the flag indicating the location of the hole. So I said "Where the heck's the hole?" He said, "Look straight ahead, you see the big trees? That's your marker. Just aim at them. They don't plant these things for nothing. There's a purpose to them." It would be nice, if only for once, common sense was the marker for how we hitch our educational wagon.

We must fight Legislature's assault on teachers

Monday morning of Thanksgiving week, I went to an urgent-care facility because of severe back pain. After an anti-inflammatory shot and with a bottle of muscle relaxers in hand, I was allowed to go home with orders not to work that day. I could not sit for long periods of time but for a grueling moment, I was able to wrestle through a newspaper article that, as I read, shook me to the core.

Upon completing the blunt article, I discovered my 18 years of seniority as a high-school teacher were gone, courtesy of our state Legislature's approval of House Bill 2011. Further, I discovered the bill "prohibits school districts from using tenure or seniority as a factor in determining which teachers can be laid off and districts no longer have to honor seniority when they rehire." In other words, a teacher can be laid off at any time without cause.

To receive such news alone and while in excruciating pain was quite difficult to take sitting down. Immediately, the analogy of the draining bathtub came to mind. First to be sucked down the drain was the housing industry, then homeowners with subprime loans, followed by the numerous job losses and now my profession and the institution I belong to has begun circling the drain.

Critics of public education have long stated that teachers need to be held accountable for student performance and that tenure makes it impossible to get rid of poor teachers. Over the years, I have worked closely with various principals both excellent and below par. The excellent principals never put up with poor teaching, tenure or not. One principal used to say, "I'd rather have knots in my stomach for a short time going through the process of getting rid of a poor teacher, than knots in my stomach knowing this teacher will be teaching my kids for years to come."

With a $3 billion projected shortfall lurking in the state budget for the upcoming fiscal year, dollars will be driving this new education model not teacher performance. This great purge coming round the bend will no doubt see experienced performing teachers departing education because school districts will get less experienced teachers at a significantly lower cost.

Because of our state's lack of commitment for long-term teachers, young promising teachers will opt to teach in other states. Class sizes and the teacher turnover rate will rise dramatically. With assessments the main focus, education in Arizona will become a sterile environment, void of personality; filled with an incredible sameness. But there is a way to plug the drain.

A campaign initiative garnering 153,365 valid petition signatures by July 1 would put a measure on the ballot aimed at overturning House Bill 2011. It would go before the voters in November. Should the ballot initiative prove successful, its binding status would prohibit the state Legislature from revisiting the issue.

As I reflect on what lies ahead, I'm reminded of a parent who asked to meet with me regarding her child's progress in my class.

She was apologetic for taking up my time. I responded, "If you don't advocate for your child's education, then who will?" This is the same question being asked of us today. The die is cast, where do you stand?

Sober reality faces public education if tax fails

"Elections have consequences," our superintendent stated recently at a staff meeting in the Tolleson Union High School District. This poignant message came after voters in our school district rejected a budget override request in March. Then came the cuts the superintendent warned would strike like a tsunami.

When the tsunami receded, it took with it 20 percent of our workforce. Swept away were teachers, secretaries, clerks, administrators, custodians, instructional aides, and counselors. And then the next wave came, sweeping away boys' and girls' athletic programs, including golf, cross country, tennis and swimming.

If anything should propel supporters of Proposition 100, the temporary 1-cent-per-dollar increase in the state sales tax, to the polls on Tuesday, it is the sobering reality of what lies ahead for many Arizona school districts if the measure fails. To date, the state Legislature has cut about $ 1.3 billion from the education budget. Two-third of the revenues raised from Prop. 100's 1-cent sales tax will be allocated toward education over the next three years.

Recently, I had the pleasure of addressing more than 400 excited and determined teachers in the Peoria Unified School District regarding Prop. 100 and a likely district budget-override election this fall. I sensed their level of concern rising in preparation to do battle in the trenches, where this war is going to be won or lost.

Peoria is a powder keg of tension sparked by board member Diane Douglas, who opposes Prop. 100 and serves as a treasurer for Ax the Tax, an organization opposed to the ballot measure. Douglas also is running for the Arizona House in District 9. In the midst of the campaign, there is a recall effort taking shape to remove Douglas from the school board.

Seeing the verbal cannonballs firing across the bow, from those for and against Prop. 100, I'm reminded of what a teacher said to me regarding her experience as she canvassed a neighborhood in search of supporters for the state sales-tax increase. The teacher informed a resident that schools are barely staying above water and that it's been this way for the past several years. She said failure of Prop. 100 will sink many school districts into the red, which could possibly cause them to either shut down or to make drastic cuts. Either one would have a profound impact on our children's education. The resident responded, "But I'm on a fixed-income." To which the teacher responded, "So are we."

Overrides needed to help keep schools afloat

At the end of a school day in mid-October, the entire staff of 180 employees at my campus was summoned to the auditorium by our superintendent. As my teaching colleagues and I filtered into the building, there was a profound sense of urgency in the air. The meeting commenced with the superintendent reading off a list of names. In a businesslike fashion she ordered, "Will the following people please stand when I call their name." Systematically, she read off names of various staff members ranging from teachers to counselors and secretaries.

Then it happened; my name was called and I rose to my feet. Looking around at the crowd of colleagues, I gauged the company I would be keeping over the next several moments. After what seemed an eternity, the list mercilessly ended at 20 names. The rest of the staff remained seated. She then asked the seated staff to take a look at the people standing and to surmise what our school would be like the following year without these staff members. She went on to say that all five high schools in our district stand to lose 20 staff members each if we are not successful in getting the budget override passed on March 9.

It was gutsy of the superintendent to use such an analogy to drive home her point. It left some teachers wondering why they weren't chosen to stand. Frankly, I'm not sure it was an honor. The point of the harsh lesson was not to divide employees but to raise their level of concern and to unite them in a common cause to do their part in passing the budget override.

Legally, the superintendent was free to speak about the override because the board had not yet officially approved a measure to seek the override. State law allows school districts to seek voter approval to increase the spending limit up to 15 percent above the current budget. This will be the case throughout Arizona on March 9 as school districts, including Tolleson Union, Dysart Unified, Deer Valley Unified, and Glendale, Laveen, Palo Verde, Union and Arlington elementary, attempt to have their requests approved by the voters.

With a $3 billion projected shortfall looming in the state budget for the next fiscal year, schools are bracing for more cuts. Last year's cuts to education were devastating. More cuts are likely. So much is at stake for our Valley schools. For some, it's securing staff positions; for others, it's preserving athletic and extracurricular programs that keep students in school. And for communities, it's keeping home values from dropping further. Voting yes for overrides will at best keep schools operating, tenuously floating above water during this current financial deluge. Considering today's harsh economic reality, it's a victory we'll take.

ELEVEN

INFORMATIONAL COLUMNS

Annoyed by military recruiters? Teachers' tour of Navy bases offers lesson

OK high school parents, 'fess up: How many of you are terribly annoyed when you receive that phone call from a recruiter who wants to enlist your son or daughter for military service? There are four branches of the military and if a recruiter from each calls your home an average of once a month, that's 48 calls a year. As a high school teacher, I hear the complaints from students as well. So when Duane Sowers, a Navy recruiter, offered me an opportunity to accompany 12 educators from Arizona and 10 from New Mexico to see the Navy and visit with our men and women in uniform, I jumped at the prospect.

Our trip would take us to Seattle, Washington. We spent the first day on Whidbey Island, which is one of the largest islands in the world and home of the Navy Prowler, a fixed wing aircraft used to stage electronic warfare by jamming radar signals. While there, we had the opportunity to speak to Navy pilots, aircraft mechanics, Navy divers, and explosive experts. We were encouraged to talk to any sailor, submariner, or pilot. Walking into an aircraft mechanics class, we conversed with students about their studies. I drew a major laugh from my colleagues when I asked students if we, as educators, had prepared them with the necessary skills for the Navy.

The fact that we hear the constant bashing of our educational system prompted me to ask the question. Almost immediately about six hands went up and when called upon each student stated that they had indeed received the proper skills to apply to their trade. Further, they wanted to thank us for what we do as educators. So, with a pat on the back, we continued on our tour.

The third day we visited Bangor Naval Base, home of the Trident nuclear submarine. The USS Henry M. Jackson is an amazing vessel. The pride of these young submariners for their ship was as evident as its nuclear missile silos. Later we had lunch with sailors to discuss their goals. While some would say they were going to make the Navy their career, others wanted to apply their newfound skills in the private sector.

The constant message that resonated from these young men and women was, despite the challenges and demands placed upon them by the Navy, they were proud to be serving our country. This adds appreciation for the arduous task of the military recruiter. Recruiters live under a constant pressure to perform. Lately, our military has not been achieving its recruitment goals. It is also apparent that military recruiters are not treated very kindly by the public and are often ridiculed. This prompts a thought: the next time you get that "annoying" phone call from a military recruiter consider the alternative—a military draft.

New Life helps abused end cycle

Imagine finding yourself in a situation where you have only moments to leave your home or risk getting killed. There's little time to pack, so you frantically gather whatever belongings you can, placing them in a plastic bag. Shortly after, you find yourself in an unfamiliar place that will harbor you for 120 days. And when your time to leave arrives you will never return home again. In 2005, 17,000 women and children in Maricopa

County found themselves in this similar situation and eventually seeking shelter.

New Life Center, a domestic violence shelter in the Southwest Valley, housed 987 women and children in 2005. Recently, along with a team of educators, I had the opportunity to tour the facility. Because of the center's commitment to providing a safe environment for its residents, its location is kept confidential.

Though many may have a perception of shelters as being rundown buildings surrounded by barbed wire and providing its residents with the bare essentials while the violent storm clears, this center is far from it. The rooms provided are similar to small patio homes, and there is a playground for the children.

Although $150,000 is budgeted annually for food, only $20,000 is spent on average because of food donations received daily from various businesses and organizations. Most residents are referred to New Life by law-enforcement services, churches and various non-profit organizations. Once women residents seeking safety are accepted by New Life Center, they enter into a program that upon completion results in over 90 percent of them not returning to the abusive environment.

The program includes education, job assistance and transportation services but, most importantly, compassion and encouragement for its tenants. "Our program model is an empowerment model," says New Life Community Development Manager Carrie Vidal Grant. Though it's a 120-day program, the average length of stay of a resident is 23 days. Staff members are quick to point out that while most batterers are men, most men are not batterers. New Life's sources of funding originate from personal and business contributions and government funding. They also accept in-kind contributions such as new car seats, hygiene products, and mostly any product having to do with everyday living.

There are some striking statistics of how domestic violence affects children.

Probably the most concerning is that 50 percent of men who abuse their wives also abuse their children. In turn, children who grow up in an abusive environment are three times more likely to abuse their own spouses and children in the future. Unfortunately, because of the lack of available space, New Life Center has to turn away three families for every one it is able to help. Perhaps this explains why the crime beat goes on and on and on.

Blog keeping readers up to date on politicians

"I found your diary underneath a tree and started reading about me." That was a popular song by '70s group Bread, and it spoke of the personal nature of a diary and the intriguing aspect of delving into someone else's thoughts. In today's internet world, online diaries, better known as blogs, are certainly the rave.

Meet Stacy Holmstedt. While working on a congressional campaign several years ago, Stacy was busy looking through old reports assessing the opponent's voting record. Thinking at first that the work would be boring, Stacy found herself actually enjoying the task. "I was surprised by how much I didn't know about my representative and his votes. So I decided to make a blog to help people find this stuff out."

One of many political blogs on the information superhighway, azcongresswatch.com, is unique in that its primary focus is to offer visitors the opportunity to see what's going on with our congressional delegation. Since its inception two years ago, azcongresswatch.com has grown steadily. The first year was incredibly slow. About the only people visiting her site were House staffers. But Stacy worked tirelessly promoting it. It now receives nearly 2000 visits a day.

At first Stacy was pretty "fired up" and "opinionated" because she had no readers and wanted to create some controversy. Since then, many sound "commenters," as Stacy refers to them, have come on board. So now she posts political items and leaves it up to her readers of various political persuasions to discuss them.

In fact, any visitor to azcongresswatch.com can easily post comments. Stacy's goal is to attract casual visitors to become interested and informed about their congressman. Candidates running for congress are also featured at azcongresswatch.com. "I get press releases from most of the candidates . . . I also get releases from John Shadegg, J.D. Hayworth, Jeff Flake, Raul Grijalva and Jon Kyl. The rest I find on Web sites," Stacy says.

When asked about the most challenging aspect of azcongresswatch. com, Stacy responded, "Right now, it's time . . . Sometimes I come home from work exhausted and think, 'I'd rather do anything but this,' but once I start working on it, it becomes fun again and suddenly it's dark outside." Of course it wouldn't be politics if there wasn't the drama that goes with it. Stacy points out, "It's been serious at times. People have gone from making jokes about weight and appearance to accusing candidates of adultery . . . . A candidate recently filed a libel suit based on comments made in my blog." Even more bizarre, Stacy's pretty sure that one of her commenters is a candidate posing as an ordinary citizen so he can attack his opponent relentlessly, and Stacy asks, "How do you handle that?" Then again, nothing but the best from some of our future leaders.

Several tips can help ward off dog attacks

Seeing it was a beautiful day, Pam Cays happily gathered her two small dogs, placed them on leashes and walked to a nearby park. What happened next still frightens her: "I saw five large dogs running loose. They quickly came toward me. Their owner was standing across the park watching. I yelled at him to get his dogs. He yelled back that they wouldn't bite. As the dogs neared, I picked up my two dogs, holding them as high as I could to protect them. The dogs then surrounded me, barking and growling. The owner would not call his dogs. He just slowly walked toward me. I yelled at him again to get his dogs. He finally called them. After several attempts, his dogs finally went to him." While a close call for Cays, others have not been as fortunate. Bob Jones, 55, of El Mirage, was attacked recently by a pit bull in a neighborhood park. Jones was bitten on the forearm and dragged about seven feet after the pit bull and Jones' beagle exchanged barks.

Spring is the season when dog attacks tend to rise. According to the Humane Society, small children, the elderly and postal carriers in this particular order make up the most frequent victims. Dog-attack victims account for one of every 20 visits to the emergency room.

Last summer, Moon Choi, a 60-year-old letter carrier, was attacked from behind while delivering mail in Torrance, Calif. A pit bull named Chucky hopped a 4-foot fence and dragged Choi to the ground. Choi suffered bites on his neck and face in what doctors deemed one of the worst attacks they had ever seen. Choi spent five days in intensive care. His injuries required 100 stitches to reattach his lip, speech therapy, plastic surgery, dental treatment, and nearly three months of rehabilitation. According to the US Postal Service, on average "10 carriers suffer dog-related injuries every delivery day." Dog bites also cost the Postal Service around $25 million a year." It is difficult to ascertain the cost of pain and suffering.

Some suggestions from the National Association of Letter Carriers for preventing dog bites apply to the civilian population as well. One, don't run past a dog. The dog's natural instinct is to chase and catch prey. Two, if a dog threatens you, don't scream. Avoid eye contact and try to remain motionless until the dog loses interest then back away slowly. Three, don't approach a strange dog, especially one that's tethered or confined. In many cases, however, dog attacks occur when the victim's dog either by its presence or by exchanging barks with an aggressive, unleashed dog sparks an attack, as was the case with Jones.

When Cays reflects back to that day when five angry dogs surrounded her while the owner passively looked on, she vowed not to be placed in that situation again. Though she still takes her pooches for walks, she is now equipped to deal with a potential dog attack, "I'm an animal lover and would never want to cause an animal pain, but from that day on, I always carry pepper spray with me when I'm out for a walk. It's sad that dogs would be the ones being sprayed, when it should be the irresponsible owner."

TWELVE

SPORTS

Glendale council has earned right to Super Bowl freebies

Not long ago I stopped by my barber for a quick trim. The TV mounted on the wall brought an interesting dose of the Oprah Winfrey show. We found it a bit humorous to actually be taking an interest in this particular segment. But why not, she was giving away DVD's, refrigerators, and big-screen TVs to every member of the audience. But Oprah was not actually giving away these items. It was the businesses doing so to advertise on this highly-rated show.

Shaking his head, my barber said, "You know, when you're rich and famous, you don't have to pay for anything. You get everything for free." No sooner had he completed his sentence, former Chicago Bulls basketball star Scottie Pippen came to mind as one who fit the pattern of entitlement. It seems word got around that Pippen did not tip waitresses when he frequented restaurants in Chicago, thereby earning him the nickname "No Tippin' Pippen." Getting things for free is a way of life for many celebrities. Imagine if you owned a night club and Brad Pitt and Angelina Jolie walked in. Would you charge them for food and drinks? Or would you use their celebrity status to boost your business. One might understand how this mentality of entitlement develops among celebrities.

So imagine my dismay when Glendale Mayor Elaine Scruggs recently announced she would probably not attend the Super Bowl because she could not afford the price of the ticket. Eventually, after much controversy and the possibility of a public relations meltdown, Scruggs was given a ticket by the Super Bowl Committee. But just as in the Mastercard commercial where some things are priceless, some things should be ticketless.

Frankly, ticketless should apply to the mayor and every member of the Glendale City Council. They should go anywhere they please and enter any suite. After all, they are the ambassadors for the city hosting this event. And they should end their visit on the sideline where no doubt many superstars will congregate. They have earned the right to a freebie and to stand on the green grass carpet. Even if it means being flanked by some celebrities the likes of "No Tippin Pippen."

Let's hope W. Valley, Cards don't rest on laurels

The Arizona Cardinals' Cinderella run to Super Bowl XLIII marked a culmination of many efforts both on and off the field. But in many respects the road to glory for the Cards and the West Valley has been eerily similar. For many years, both languished in the abyss of inequality, much like a poor stepchild. The West Valley's anemic political strength and lack of comprehensive leadership led to its falling behind the East Valley in both transportation and infrastructure funding, affecting its growth and quality of life.

Without a stadium of its own for nearly twenty years, the Cardinals lacked the revenue stream to put a quality team on the field. This history of futility for both the West Valley and the Cards created a negative perception among critics and various media that they would never be able to measure up. In many respects this perception still exists today. For the West Valley, no more was this evident than when it was a finalist with Tempe in the competition to land the new Cardinals stadium approved by Maricopa County voters in 2000.

In several news segments comparing both sites, Tempe was featured with all its glamour and amenities. For the West Valley, there was just a close-up shot of a cotton field and the sound of crickets mixed with depressing silence. There was even negative commentary about the odor of fertilizer used in nearby fields. Tempe would win the stadium sweepstakes, but the city ran into difficulties, despite all of the advantages given to it by state, regional and local leaders. In a stroke of fate's compassion, combined with tireless leadership of our community leaders, the stadium would come to the West Valley. A new era began.

This fortunate circumstance led to new revenue streams for the Cards and the West Valley, proving that all each needed was the opportunity to compete. This, in turn, spawned a cultural change. But despite the recent success, it does beg the question: Where do we go from here? How do we in the West Valley want to define ourselves for the future? We have a state-of-the-art hockey and entertainment facility, two new Major League Baseball spring-training sites, a state of the art cancer medical center, future Fiesta Bowls, a possible 600—room casino resort and another hosting of a Super Bowl in 2013 as well as the firm belief in future Super Bowl appearances for the Cards. Becoming a sports Mecca may be the linchpin to propel the West Valley into a better quality of life for its residents by spurring future benefits such as light rail, high-tech jobs, a thriving education, improved health care, and just downright community fun.

Conflict is said to be one of eight ingredients to creating a vibrant culture. The West Valley and the Cardinals have seen their fair share of the worst conflict can offer. Perhaps these trials of adversity explain why each has performed incredibly well on the new stage. There is still work to be done. Let's hope both the West Valley and the Cardinals choose not to rest on their laurels and continue to usher in a new dawn.

THIRTEEN

TEEN CHALLENGES

Teens engaged in 'sexting' could find futures derailed

Our nation's current economic woes may not be what keep teens from securing a promising career. It may very well be a moment of indiscretion posted on cyberspace. It's called "sexting": sending nude or semi-nude photos from cellphone to cellphone. Usually it involves the person text-messaging nude pictures of themselves to someone else.

During an interview on a Cincinnati television station in May 2008, 18-year-old Jessica Logan told her story about the time she text-messaged nude photos of herself to her boyfriend. After they broke up, the boyfriend circulated her photos to friends at school. As a result, she endured mocking and harassment from her peers. Jessica went public to try to prevent other teens from following in her footsteps. Unfortunately, the harassment at school proved too much for Jessica to bear. Two months after the interview, she committed suicide by hanging herself in her bedroom.

Sexters are also finding themselves in legal trouble because it is considered child pornography in many states if a minor sends nude photos electronically. If convicted, it could mean jail time and having to register as a sex offender. According to a recent survey conducted by the National Campaign to Prevent Teen and Unplanned Pregnancy, 20 percent of teens have either sent or posted nude or semi-nude pictures or even a video of themselves. Other survey results: 39 percent of all teens and 59 percent of all young adults are sending or posting sexually suggestive messages; 25 percent of teen girls and 33 percent of teen boys say they have received nude or semi-nude pictures originally meant for someone else.

Complicating matters further is that many of these images end up posted on social network sites such as MySpace and Facebook. These are the very sites prospective universities and employers are using as tools to assess the character of potential candidates to their programs and institutions. One common denominator suggests the younger children begin texting, the more likely they will participate in some form of sexting. The NCPTUP offers some tips to help parents communicate with their children about sexting:

- Know who your kids are communicating with.
- Consider limitations on electronic communication such as taking the laptop out of their bedroom before they go to bed.
- Be aware of what your teens are posting publicly, and set expectations by making sure you are clear with your teen about what you consider appropriate "electronic" behavior.

Probably the most important tip is to talk to your kids about what they are doing in cyberspace and explain the short—and long-term consequences of their actions. Otherwise, a teen may soon discover that their dream of that promising career may have already ended before it ever began.

Cell phone text messaging: Latest classroom disruption

Fifteen years ago, when I was preparing to become a high school teacher, I was introduced to a book written by Dr. Frederick Jones titled *Positive Classroom Discipline* that describes the different types of students one might encounter in the classroom. I also found his view on classroom management quite compelling. Jones believed that the major threat to creating a positive learning environment was not the disruptive student whose poor behavior was obvious to the teacher, but the silent disruption that quite often goes unnoticed. He believed that successful teachers had become effective by developing "eyes on the back of their heads," spotting those silent disruptions and dealing with them before they got out of hand. Cell phone text messaging has become the new silent disruption infiltrating high school classrooms. Teens are fast becoming experts of covertly texting one another during class.

Megan Raulston, a recent high school graduate in the West Valley, would text message an average 1,500 times per month. "It's the greatest thing in the world! It's easy for you to get in touch with your friends anytime," she says. Megan estimates that 50 percent of the text messages she sent or received were during class. Conversations ranged from boy talk to deciding which weekend party to attend. Text messaging also has an impact on academic integrity, as some students use this practice to cheat on exams.

Some initial studies are suggesting that the earlier teens begin text messaging, the more likely they are to engage in sex because, as the texting experience progresses, it becomes easier for teens to become more daring and sexually graphic with their conversations. Text messaging can also be expensive. Some cases have teens running bills up as high as $800.

Since the start of another school year has arrived, it is important for parents to realize the distractions text messaging might pose for their children and how it could ultimately affect their performance in school and on standardized tests such as AIMS. If parents are adamant about providing their children with cell phones, they might want to forgo the text messaging feature.

As gang activity rises . . . rise again to snuff it

Yogi Berra's famous quote "it's déjà vu all over again" was likely meant as a humorous pun. But, in many regards, there is a sad truth to it, as well, particularly when it comes to gangs. Not long ago, I took part in a meeting about the recent escalation of gang activity in the West Valley. As I listened to the discussion about the allure of gangs and how to spot gang activities in neighborhoods, I realized very little has changed since I worked security at a local high school from 1989 to 1992. During this time, a major campus disruption occurred after a student, who was a member of a gang, was killed during a gun battle in the parking lot of a popular dance club.

Many of the gangs from that time are still around today. They never left. They were just held in check for a while. Law-enforcement officials are alarmed by the increase in gang violence—the drive-by shootings, vicious competition for territory and horrific homicides. They have been meeting monthly to share information regarding gang activity and to devise a strategy to eradicate gangs and the crimes associated with them. Police departments from Glendale, El Mirage, Surprise, Goodyear, as well as the FBI, personnel from neighboring prisons and every facet of law enforcement are taking part in these meetings in Avondale.

Many gangs seek validation. For this reason, it would not be proper to name them publicly. However, it would be wise to understand why these groups exist in our society. One reason gangs exist is it gives the members a sense of family or belonging. There is also the rush of excitement in belonging to a gang, and the opportunity to make money by taking part in crimes of profit such as drug dealing. And, sadly, some simply grow up in a family of gang members and this type of life is all they know.

The most overt sign of emerging gang activity in a community is when structures, buildings, and abandoned homes begin falling victim to graffiti. Some of the tools being deployed in the West Valley to combat the problem are mobile cameras positioned to cover an area prone to graffiti. Once a sensor in the camera is set off, it calls a cell phone monitored by law enforcement. Every city in the West Valley provides a graffiti hotline number on its Web site. It is vital that graffiti comes down as soon as it goes up in a neighborhood, law-enforcement officials say.

While Yogi Berra's "déjà vu all over again" remains apropos regarding the reemergence of gangs in the West Valley, it can also apply when we get to see them severely diminished once again.

FOURTEEN

THE SLIPPERY SLOPE

It's time to get angry about photo-radar abuse

Mick and Jeff, two colleagues of mine, were golfing some time back. Mick was angry about some issue at work. But what made him most angry was that Jeff wasn't miffed about the issue at all. Because of Mick's frustration, he made it his mission to see Jeff angry by the end of the ninth hole. Don't know whether he succeeded, but I can surely relate to Mick's frustration. I feel it when I see the love affair our elected officials are having with photo-radar enforcement and the $90 million annual cash cow it's quickly becoming, I'm amazed that the public seems to be taking this concept in stride.

Perhaps when more people start falling prey to this unforgiving technology and when folks catch wind of what's coming down the line in the near future regarding new photo-radar technology, the angry meter will begin to rise. To see what lies ahead, we need not look any further than Europe. For example, in Spain, photo-enforcement cameras mounted on helicopters will soon be hitting the air. Unlike what we have in a few of our states, where police helicopters inform law-enforcement officers on the ground with the estimated speed of a vehicle in question, helicopters in Spain will operate just like the cameras on the ground, homing in with radar on vehicle license plates and automatically generating a citation in the mail to the offending motorist.

Even in Australia, cameras installed on stop signs are ticketing drivers for failing to make a complete stop. Other photo-radar enforcement technology can detect auto emissions from tail pipes and vehicle parking overstays, even if by 1 minute.

But of all the possible ways for government to extract money from you through the use of photo-radar technology, the most likely to be in our midst is the new line of photo-enforcement cameras currently being offered by German company ProContour. These are equipped with the ability to assess tire tread wear. When deployed, European motorists driving on tires worn beyond factory recommendations will receive a citation in the mail equivalent to $160.

Currently, Arizona is the only state taking photo-enforcement statewide with 100 stationary and mobile cameras on our interstates and many more deployed in our cities and neighborhoods. When it comes to the issue of photo-radar enforcement, I won't be satisfied until you're not satisfied. So, where are you on the angry meter?

More to red-light cameras than proponents reveal

Since the City of Avondale installed red-light cameras at the intersection of McDowell and Dysart roads, have you found yourself taking alternate routes whenever possible? I must confess that I have. I've seen the red-carpet treatment awaiting red-light runners during the warning period, which recently lapsed. When cameras flash, it's like the paparazzi at the Oscars, even in the daytime. At this point, $140 citations will be issued to red-light runners.

Now I know what many of you are thinking: "Hey Randy, obey the law!' and you have nothing to worry about. Misjudging the length of a yellow light is not what concerns me; keeping the rear of my car intact does. Proponents of red-light cameras maintain that they reduce accidents. While on the surface this point of view seems logical, digging deeper you may find some surprising results.

According to studies in California and Canada, rear-end collisions increased at intersections where red-light cameras were installed. In some cases, they even doubled. In fact, Virginia, North Carolina and Australia have come to the same conclusion. Red-light cameras are also involved in a few legal entanglements. Recently in Minneapolis, the American Civil Liberties Union brought a suit against photo enforcement on the basis that it violates citizens' right to due process. Judge Mark S. Wernick agreed and declared red-light cameras as well as speed cameras unconstitutional. In Steubenville, Ohio, Judge David E. Henderson also struck down red-light cameras. However, he took it a step further. He issued an order for Steubenville to refund approximately 4,000 tickets at $85 each.

Unlike other states, photo enforcement has not been profitable in Arizona. Phoenix, on average, loses more than $300,000 annually. Last year, Mesa reported a loss of more than $220,000. Contrasting other states that pay a flat fee to red-light camera vendors, Arizona pays vendors on a per-citation basis.

Avondale is wise for allowing itself a one-year period to study the results of red-light cameras. When determining their future, the amount of accidents should be a fundamental part of the criteria. But so should the impact red-light cameras may pose on businesses and whether photo enforcement shifts the traffic burden to other areas and increases commute time. Meantime, while Avondale ponders the future of red-light cameras, my weekend drives to visit Mom in Tolleson will continue to go by way of Mississippi.

Better engineering, fewer red-light woes

I often wonder if, in our haste to solve problems, we wind up making them worse. If focusing on good things produces good things then wouldn't it be logical that the same would occur if we focused on bad things? For example, does the war on drugs produce more drugs or does the war on terror produce more terrorists?

This is not to say we shouldn't act to prevent bad things from occurring, but should they become our obsession to the extent that we risk producing more of them?

Red-light cameras are currently the rage in cities across Maricopa County. The obvious concerns are red-light runners and that mental image they produce of a driver barreling across an intersection at a high rate of speed inflecting great human damage upon the innocent. So, the focus becomes red-light runners and how we must act to stop them. But have red-light runners become our obsession to the extent that we are producing more of them? Is a red-light camera going to stop that red-light runner we most fear? And do red-light cameras produce more red-light runners and in some cases more accidents?

During a six month period in 2006, Avondale's red-light cameras at two intersections on Dysart Road issued 2,400 citations. Approximately 70 percent of the citations were issued to drivers who failed to make a full stop before turning right at a red light. One intersection saw a drop in accidents while the other an increase. National Motorists Association, an organization that opposes photo enforcement believes red-light cameras not only fail to work but are counterproductive. NMA maintains that if "intersections are properly designed, and signals are properly installed and timed, red-light running is reduced to inconsequential levels." This approach makes traffic engineering safety the focus, not red-light runners.

According to NMA, by enlarging traffic light lenses, re-striping left turn lanes, re-timing traffic signals and including a brief period where the lights in all directions are red after the yellow light "phases out," communities will see a reduction in red light violations. So confident is NMA that it has offered any city in America a $10,000 challenge. "We will guarantee a *minimum* 50-percent reduction in red-light violations through the application of engineering solutions. If our recommendations fail . . . we will pay the community $10,000." But if their engineering recommendations succeed, the city must "scrap its ticket camera program."

With a recent measure in the State Legislature making auto owners, not drivers, liable for red-light violations and which prompted concern among members of the Avondale City Council, maybe it's time for Avondale to take up NMA's $10,000 challenge. By accepting the challenge and redirecting the focus from red-light runners to traffic engineering safety, the best case scenario is NMA's $10,000 challenge succeeds, resulting in a reduction of red-light violations and scrapping of the cameras. For which I'll even kick in the price of a citation.

Will pensions come crashing down?

His hands nervously toggled the instruments in the cockpit of the Boeing 747 he was piloting. He had made this trek from the Far East to San Francisco countless times before. But finality was beginning to set in on Captain Millard "Mill" Kerr. His life flashed before his eyes. Soon, his focus became the approaching runway. It seemed to take an eternity, but finally the Boeing's tires made contact with the asphalt. Mill breathed a sigh of relief.

A gamut of emotions overtook him. In the cockpit he anxiously removed his uniform coat and replaced it with a casual shirt. As he stepped into the cabin of the plane, his wife, Mary Jo, greeted him. Thirty-two years of service as a pilot for United Airlines had come to a close. "That's it. I'm hanging it up," he thought, as he could hardly wait to start his new life. He's never thought that flying 747s for a living was anything to boast about. "I just did what I did . . . It was no big deal."

Since that special day in March of 1994, Mill, who resides in Sun City West, has spent his time joyously working as a volunteer chaplain at Del Webb Hospital and also volunteering at Habitat for Humanity. Lately however, Mill has become concerned about United Airlines defaulting on its $9 billion employee pension plan, leaving the federal government's Pension Benefit Guarantee Corp. to assume the debt. He worries about the impact this may have on his pension, but he also worries for his friends at United who have since retired and whose pensions are at risk as well. The Pension Benefit Guarantee Corp. has seen a rise in corporate pension defaults and is currently $23 billion in debt. This current trend may lead to a domino effect as companies try to cut overhead costs, thus confirming that retirees have become fair game in this age of downsizing.

Surprisingly Mill isn't bitter. At 71 he is preparing for a worst-case scenario. "Change is inevitable," he says, adding, "We have to be willing to change when the time comes." He recently obtained a real estate license (just in case) and says that if his pension is severely affected, he and Mary Jo will have to downsize their lifestyle. This also means he will have to replace his casual shirt for a Realtor's coat!

Medical marijuana initiative may open Pandora's box

If you think the political landscape has changed dramatically in Arizona since Senate Bill 1070 came into the picture, consider how radically different the physical landscape will appear to Arizonans should voters approve in November Proposition

203, the medical-marijuana initiative. If the measure passes, 120 dispensaries would be operating throughout Arizona offering various types of marijuana to patients that receive a doctor's recommendation for illnesses such as cancer, muscular sclerosis, AIDS and other diseases deemed chronic or terminal. Patients living farther than 25 miles from a dispensary would be able to grow their own supply. By law, physicians are prohibited from writing prescriptions for marijuana. The only way around this legal hurdle is for doctors to write "recommendations" instead of prescriptions.

Andrew Myers from the Arizona Medical Marijuana Policy Project was a guest recently on my radio program, "From the Roots Up." He acknowledges that California and Colorado have had their share of dispensary problems, but he believes Prop. 203 addresses many of the shortcomings these states have encountered because Prop. 203 comes with more regulations.

California's poorly crafted medical-marijuana program has resulted in a de facto legalization of marijuana in the Golden State, Meyers said. Two-third of Californians receiving medical marijuana are under 35, prompting critics to claim that access to doctor recommendations for medical marijuana is just too easy. They say it's a sham in that what has happened is the word "medical" has been added to marijuana. Under Prop. 203, there are no requirements for certification for employees at dispensaries. Patients will be allowed 2.5 ounces of marijuana every 14 days, which is about five to 14 joints per day. Many patients choose to ingest marijuana in their food. Myers said much can be learned from mistakes made in California and Colorado. (Colorado services 60,000 patients.) He is confident Arizona would not follow in the same path and would be a positive model for other states to follow regarding how to effectively conduct a medical-marijuana program.

I have strong reservations about Prop. 203. Conceptually, I believe in the sanctity of patient-doctor privacy. If a medical decision is made to give someone terminally or chronically ill access to medical marijuana, it should be handled in the same manner as with any prescription, not fall onto a loosely conceived doctor-recommendation policy. Perhaps this is why dispensaries in California and Colorado have had their share of problems.

Also difficult to accept is the prospect that our young ones might be able to legally attain access to this pure type of marijuana, which is 25 times more potent than pot was in the 1960s. Despite assurances that medical marijuana in Arizona would be different compared with California and Colorado, there is still so much that can go wrong. If Prop. 203 passes, we may well be opening Pandora's box.

FIFTEEN

OFFBEAT STORIES

Lent perfect time to try Tolleson fish restaurant

(Ash Wednesday starts busy month for Pete's)

Ash Wednesday is today, marking the beginning of the Lenten season for many Christians throughout the world. Although the method of observation varies from one denomination to another, to many Christians, Lent is a time for reflection and abstaining from meat on Fridays. This act of forgoing continues until the Saturday before Easter. This 40-day period is marked by sunrise church services and Friday fish fries. It is also the time many in the Southwest Valley flock to Pete's Fish & Chips in Tolleson to partake in their seafood and famous Pete's sauce.

Pete's, 9309 W. Van Buren St., has flourished for more than 50 years, and despite the changing times, it continues with its simple tradition of serving its clientele much in the same manner it did 50 years ago: by screaming out order numbers through a small screen window. Pete's is also well-known for its non-seafood items, such as the Super Burger and the Dixie Dog, which is a breaded hot dog. My brother, Rick, still prides himself as being the first customer of the Monster Burger.

After church service several years ago, I stopped by Pete's on Ash Wednesday to place an order. The drive-through line wrapped around the parking lot like a giant anaconda. The size of the walk-up crowd resembled a pack of concertgoers eager for tickets. Albert Hernandez, a short-order cook at the time, came over to give me a quick hello. Shaking his head in wonder, he said, "It's amazing! We've only sold one hamburger today. Everything else has been seafood." In fact, this is the time of year when most of the meat simply remains in the freezer.

"It's chaotic. It stays busy every day from Ash Wednesday until Easter because a lot of people give up meat not just on Fridays but every day during Lent," assistant manager Viviana Del Toro said. Worldwide, the Jewish High Holy Days and Islam's Ramadan are also seasons observed in much the same fashion Christians observe Lent: by fasting, praying and abstaining from certain types of food. Interestingly, despite the state of our world, where pride rules the day, this is the season for placing pride on the shelf, reflecting on one's faith and finding victory in surrendering.

Monument atop hill reminds that past shapes us today

As a child playing football in the streets of my neighborhood, I would gaze at the Estrella Mountains to the south and naively believed that the other side was Mexico. I imagined people riding on horseback and stagecoaches kicking up dust in peaceful rustic pueblos. Turns out my childhood vision was not that far off the beaten path. History tells us that the Estrellas were indeed Mexican territory at one time. The United States bought the land from Mexico in 1853 in a land deal known as the Gadsden Purchase. For $10 million, the United States gained territory stretching from southern Arizona to El Paso. It encompassed approximately 30,000 square miles. Tucson was part of the deal. Before the purchase, our border with Mexico was at the Gila River, which stretches north of the Estrellas through the West

Valley including Tolleson, Avondale, Goodyear and Buckeye. The Gila travels west and eventually connects with the Colorado River in Southern California.

But, why the Gadsden Purchase? President Franklin Pierce saw the territory as vital to the creation of a southern transcontinental railway that would connect to California. This helps explain why the southern boundary line of Arizona curves upward toward California instead of a straight line. Tall-tale stories abound regarding drunken surveyors drawing the Arizona boundary line crooked is obviously not the case. Interestingly, had the agreement allowed the boundary line to be drawn straight, Arizona would today be basking with beach front property including Rocky Point. America had no desire to go further south; one reason was the concern for providing adequate security from Indian attacks. The Gadsden Purchase ushered in commercial and social life to a land deemed "barren and uninhabitable." It also solidified America's final boundary.

Just east of Phoenix International Raceway in Avondale stands a hill about 300 ft. high known to many locals as Monument. It is the point where intense government surveying took place on the tiny mountain's summit in 1851, two years before the Gadsden Purchase. The Department of the Interior declared the tiny mountain summit a national land mark and placed a monument on the very spot where the surveying took place.

Recently, I trekked up the rugged hill of loose rock with a colleague. I had been to the summit once before many years back. Two nice folks on horseback assured us that the monument was still there. Upon reaching the summit, I was pleased to see the monument in relatively good condition. Standing on the tiny mountain and looking in every direction, history's presence came to life. As I gazed at the Gila River below, I wondered how different life would be were it still the border today. A circling flock of buzzards reminded me just how natural and pristine much of the area remains.

I also marveled at the great view the hill provides of the race track at PIR. Which elicits this thought: The next time you're at the race track, look east to a nearby tiny mountain sitting honorably as a reminder of a past that shapes who we are today, Americans with so much in common.

Jolly Old Elf Drove a Cop Car

T'was a cold Christmas day in 2003,
At St. Thomas Aquinas church were we three,
Myself, wife Inez and young daughter Giselle
Sang songs of white Christmas—then rang a church bell.
Service was over, so we rushed to our car,
But the traffic was heavy, and the walk seemed quite far.
As our car came in view something didn't seem right
And suddenly this scene much gave us a fright.
There was glass on the ground, and what seemed a big curse
Car thieves had made off with Giselle's tiny purse!
The gravity of the moment tore into Giselle,
Signaling strongly that things were not well,
Trembling she asked "Why are there scrooges Dad?"
Her words left me searching and feeling quite bad.
Such a tragic event, one can't explain it away—
Especially when it's happened on Christmas day.
As she cried and shed tears, the likes never heard before
I grew angry, longing to settle the score;
Suddenly! From afar came a car with blue flashing lights
And out came a cop prepared for the fight
No it wasn't a fight to make the thieves pay
T'was to make Giselle happy again this Christmas Day.
Derrick Montgomery was the officer's name

Confidence and discipline came along with his fame
As he inspected the crime scene I couldn't help but see
His uniform was different, Yes! It glistened with glee!
But what of his outfit would make scrooges scat?
T'il it finally struck me; He wore Santa's hat!
He bent down with a frown and a strong cop's demeanor
With a wallop he did say, with a voice growing meaner,
"It wasn't right what those thieves took away,
But don't let them ruin Christmas; do you hear what I say?"
Then he led her to the car with blue flashing lights
Stocked with gifts from some elves, much to our delight.
With a smile and a jolly laugh just like St. Nick
The cop gave Giselle a gift which he let her pick.
T'would seem this Christmas took a big turn
When Giselle smiled and laughed again, did a lesson we learn:
To be thankful for the good deeds that others do
And not let scrooges win, Oh how this is true!
We will never forget how Santa came to us this way
In the form of a cop who saved Christmas that day.

SIXTEEN

WHAT'S RACE GOT TO DO WITH IT?

Little Johnny at the Principal's Office

In the late 1940's, Johnny, a student at Tolleson Elementary School, sat nervously in Principal Kenneth Dyer's office anxiously awaiting the consequence for his defiant behavior. Soon a heated exchange of words commenced between Johnny and the principal, ending with Dyer's angry declaration, "Over my dead body will I desegregate this school!" For generations, the Tolleson Elementary School Board and administration practiced segregation using the Plessy v. Ferguson court case as justification for instituting such policies under the guise of 'separate but equal.' The separation of nearly 300 Hispanic students from their Anglo counterparts was hardly equal. Hispanics could not enjoy the luxuries of a cafeteria, playground or auditorium which the Anglo school possessed.

So, Johnny, 16 years old at the time, set out to end the practice of segregation at his school. He gathered support from courageous locals who met regularly to plan a course of action. Johnny would inform the community of upcoming meetings by screaming announcements to residents from a bull horn while riding on the back of a pickup truck. Eventually, they raised enough money to secure some attorneys to handle their case. The fight to desegregate the Tolleson Elementary Schools began with a defiant teenager but would end in the courts where adults from opposing sides would battle to make their case.

In 1950, the group filed suit against the Tolleson Elementary School Board of Trustees eventually known as the court case Gonzales v. Sheely. In 1951, the U.S. District Court of Arizona ordered the Tolleson Elementary School District to desegregate. In 1999, Tolleson Elementary School was named after Porfirio Gonzales, who bravely inked his name—along with Faustino Curiel, a community member—as plaintiff in the case amidst the threat of ostracism from the community.

On March 25, 2011, a dedication ceremony was held at Porfirio Gonzales Elementary School in Tolleson, to honor the courageous individuals that fought gallantly to end segregation at the Tolleson elementary schools. The 15 individuals' names are engraved on a memorial called, "The Legacy of Courage".

The memorial wall bears the names of John "Juan" Camacho, Cruz Gonzalez de Contreras, Faustino Curiel, Isauro & Lupe Favela, Angelita Fuentes, Trinidad Gem, Jr., Joe Gonzales, Porfirio H. Gonzales, Patsy Murrieta, Manuel Peña, Sr., and Manuel "Lito" Peña, Jr.: Attorneys Ralph C. Estrada, Greg Garcia, and A.L. Wirin.

Yes, Johnny, the defiant student is my uncle John "Juan" Camacho. He currently resides in San Jose, California. He is now a sprightly 77. When I informed him of the dedication ceremony he was very moved by the effort. What is most impressive about this group's achievement is that it helped set the stage for the famous Supreme Court case Brown v. Board of Education of 1954, which declared racial segregation of schools unconstitutional. His only concern is that everyone who played a role in the effort be recognized properly. The Legacy of Courage Memorial Wall is a good start. It states in part:

"In 1949, a young, defiant voice cried out against an unjust policy, sowing a seed of courage among many to stand as one against an unlawful act of discrimination. Their only grievance was to be treated equal under the law . . . . In 1950, parents filed a suit against the Tolleson Elementary School Board of Trustees . . . . On March 26, 1951, the United States District Court of Arizona ordered the Tolleson Elementary School District to desegregate . . . . This memorial is dedicated to all the brave individuals that fought with great courage and humility to bring an end to the segregation of the Tolleson Elementary Schools . . . . Their legacy is a firm reminder that the fight for social justice continues."

Do you ever feel sorry for White people?

In the summer of 2008, I posed a question to a political counterpart that intrigued her so much, she did not answer immediately. She was raised on a reservation in a rural part of Arizona and grew up without plumbing or electricity in her home. One night we were making our way from a Fourth of July campaign event in Flagstaff to another in Prescott. I was driving while she worked on her laptop. We were making our way through the back mountains of Prescott when I posed a question that perplexed her. I asked, "Do you ever feel sorry for white people?" She thought hard but did not answer my question. I left well enough alone.

Several weeks later, we were making our trip back through the same area. The scene was nearly identical to the time when I had posed the question. She then said, "By the way, I do feel sorry for white people!" (Now, the question I have asked many is why did I ask this question? And why did she answer yes?) Imagine, a Hispanic growing up working in the onion fields to help his family make ends meet and a Native-American who grew up in extreme poverty feeling sorry for white people. What is that all about?

Nothing justified my question more than the Shirley Sherrod incident which happened in the summer of 2010. Here was an African-American woman on YouTube delivering a speech to a predominantly black audience of the N.A.A.C.P about the time when a white couple came to her for help because they were about to lose their farm. Sherrod worked for the Department of Agriculture. She went on to say that the prospect of helping this white couple was a sense of irony for her.

Shirley grew up on a farm in Baker County in the state of Georgia. She was one of six girls in her family. Her father wanted a son so badly that he gave each of the girls a boy's nickname. Shirley's nickname was Bill. They grew turnips and peanuts for the most part. Shirley could not wait to head north for college because she believed things would be better there. During her senior year of high school, Shirley's father was killed by a white man. During those days in the '40s and '50s, a white man killing a black man would not be convicted of murder in Baker County. It would be the same in the case of Shirley's father. Despite the testimony of three witnesses to the murder, an all-white grand jury refused to convict the accused killer.

So, one might understand her anger towards a particular race and a rigged judicial system which favored one race over the other. She goes on to explain how she had no desire to help the white couple who had come seeking assistance to save their farm. So the video ends with Sherrod making the statement, "So I didn't give him the full force of what I could do." But what no one realized at the time was that there was more to the video. The blogger, Andrew Breitbart, a person of questionable character, released the video portion only to that point, claiming that the video of Sherrod's speech had arrived to him that way. When word got to Agriculture Secretary Tom Vilsack of Sherrod's supposed comments, he ordered her immediate supervisor to fire Sherrod. In their haste to get rid of Sherrod and avoid a public relations nightmare, her supervisor contacted Sherrod on her cell phone while she was on the road conducting business for the Agriculture Department. She was ordered to pull over to the side of the road and to text in her resignation, which she did.

Meantime, CNN talk-show host Rick Sanchez located the farmer couple Sherrod had mentioned in her story. When asked to describe what had happened to them during the time they met Sherrod, their first statement was, "Shirley Sherrod is our friend." They went on to recount how Sherrod had saved their farm many years ago by connecting them with the right people and seeing things through with them every step of the way.

Shortly after the couple's interview, Sherrod started to make her way on the airwaves to tell her side of the story. When the full version of her speech was played—which had always been available on YouTube—it was apparent the reason Sherrod had shared this story was because up until that point in her life, she had always viewed poverty as a problem for minorities exclusively. What she had learned as she explains is that poverty and lack of access for assistance is a challenge for Americans from all walks of life; even 'white people'. This experience had also helped her come to grips with the race issue.

The Obama administration offered Sherrod her job back but she respectfully refused. It seems there was plenty of blame to go around regarding how this matter was handled; but through it all when early perceptions of Shirley Sherrod were that she was looking to stick it to someone because they were white, she remained on the high road even after she was ordered to take the low road of others to tender her resignation.

BIBLIOGRAPHY

It's a cliché to call someone a person of integrity, but those of us who know Randy Camacho, a native of Arizona, can attest that he truly is a man of integrity, governed by his principles and not his circumstances. Randy's circumstances haven't always been easy.

He spent much of his childhood working in the onion fields as a farm-laborer helping his family make ends meet. He recalls being picked up after Little League games by his brother in an onion-hauling truck where they would spend the night in the fields in order to jockey to be one of the first trucks loaded at sun up.

Perhaps Randy's habit of getting up early and working hard as a youngster enabled him to have a notable high school career. He participated in basketball and baseball, became student body president, won the *Outstanding Senior Boy* award, and was the first non-football player in Tolleson High School's 50-year history to be chosen homecoming king.

After high school, Randy worked and eventually went into business owning a video-appliance store and an auto-upholstery shop. After some difficult setbacks, he became determined to return to college; while working full-time during the day, he attended school in the evenings and weekends.

In 1992, Randy earned his Bachelor's degree from Ottawa University and became a Social Studies teacher at Westview

High School. He went on to receive a Master of Arts degree in Administration and Supervision at the University of Phoenix in 1995.

Randy is married to Inez, his wife of 23 years, and has two wonderful daughters, Alexzandria and Giselle and two grandchildren, Nadia and Tavier.

A former congressional candidate, Randy has served as a political consultant, community columnist for the *Arizona Republic* and local radio talk show host.

Randy knows what it means to be refined by hardship and driven by the American Dream. He believes in hard work, teamwork and the value of an education. He is an example to his peers and a role model to the youth he mentors. His life is an extension of who he is; a man of integrity.

Lynn Caddell,
Longtime Friend
Bremerton, Washington